THE 5TH SEED

THE 5TH SEED

MERCEDES BLEU

To order additional copies of this book, contact:
Xlibris Corporation
1-888-795-4274
www.Xlibris.com
Orders@Xlibris.com
28974

CONTENTS

*This book I dedicate to Mama and her family,
especially the kids, the seeds of life.*

*Many thanks to everyone at forty-four, who encouraged
and assisted me in making Mama's life
live through words.*

*Thanks to L. Griffin, PhD, and J. Pruett, editor,
for their friendship, guidance, and love.*

*Special thanks to Lucy Hopkins, for
keeping it moving and making it fun.
You are a blessing!*

ACKNOWLEDGMENTS

For all of Mama's seeds, I dedicate her words, thoughts, and deeds. To one great lady who by God's choice became my mother, I thank you, Mama. Am I a lucky seed or what? It is because of her love, easy spirit, and unending friendship that I *am*. These special qualities brought me from Mama's little baby to Mama's big baby. My dad was tickling, loving, and hugging special. His 50 percent contribution was all good, strong, and sure. I thank God he was there to keep me in line.

It was all those soft, warm, fuzzy, insightful intangibles my mother instilled in me that need to be shared. It was the real stuff like her compassion, caring, listening, understanding, hearing, laughing, peace, faith, and love.

Where did she learn to be available, understanding, patient, and encouraging to six different personalities at one time and in one place? How, in a time before TV and documentaries, did she acquire the wisdom and commitment? Her desire was to consistently treat each child as though he or she were her only child. She believed in me until I believed in myself. Mama always wanted to be a schoolteacher. For that reason, I share her teaching and her humor with this "too busy for a family" world. In my opinion, she fulfilled her dream. So learn this if no more, your family is uniquely yours good, bad or indifferent; they are yours. It's up to each person to sift through all that is available and take only those things that enhance the total individual.

It's not what's in a person's house that makes it a home; it's that special feeling when one enters his own house. It's the love that one feels for the people inside that makes it a home. It's what's in the heart that makes one happy, and it's all about happiness. If one's family was, is, or will be different from mine, we should thank our parents for giving us the gift of life because God's gift to you is life; what you do with it is your gift to God.

So as Mom says, keep living and keep laughing, for these are the keys for longevity. She is ninety-four, so know that I believe her. The only way I know to repay my parents and theirs and their parents before them is to live life and love it.

Reader, Welcome to My World

If you are like who I used to be, the only books you read were how-to books, required college courses, or time-filling fiction. Well, this is a totally unique experience! You are going to relax, unwind, relate, laugh, cry, and think. So get a cup of coffee, tea, spirits, or popcorn. Find a special place in your car, on your porch, in the park, in the bed, in an easy chair, in an airplane, or at the office.

Look! Let's not put off the greatest trip until some other time. If you don't see yourself in these pages, you will see people you know and love.

The Way It Was!

This is the true story of a very special baby who grows up and touches everyone she meets, and if you'll let her, she will touch even you. In her thirty-sixth year of life, she touches me. I am a baby in her future living now in the genes of a family who came before me. First, let's go back in time and live life with her.

The year is 1907. The place is Clover, South Carolina. It is February 20. This is the day she is born. Her parents, Cornellius and Beerman Bryant, are born here, grow up here, and raise their family here. The Bryants have a son, Jay Van, who is almost five years old. They name their new daughter Cynthia. Their dream of one son and one daughter has come true.

This town called Clover is so small that it should be called *over* because before anyone gets in it, it's over. Clover is a few short streets of whitewashed homes and churches. The tree-lined streets fade into endless pastures of grazing cows and horses. A short walk beyond the large farms is downtown Clover. On one side of Main Street are a drugstore, general store, the Bank of Clover, the post office, and carriage shop. Katie's Kettle is the town cafe; Ike's Barbershop, Jenkin's Funeral Home, and the town presser make up the other side of the street. A small hospital and Clover Center School face Main Street. On the lawn of the small country school, a gold Liberty Bell can be seen glowing in the noonday sun. A new crisp flag flies high on a flagpole at the entrance of the schoolyard. Through the open windows of the school comes the sweet sound of children reciting the pledge of allegiance. In the distance, the sound of the only train that stops in Clover each day announces its arrival. At the time Cynthia is born, Clover is so small that homes don't use mailing addresses. Mail is delivered based on post-office box number. The local post office is the size of a baby's room. Beerman is Clover's first Afro-American postmaster and mailman. He is a tall slim man, who spends much of his day talking to friends and neighbors as he delivers their mail. People look forward to his morning visits with coffee or a cool drink.

The Bryant home is a large white house with a white picket fence. Beautiful flowers, fruit trees, rosebushes, and grapevines cover the space between green grass and shade trees.

I hear hundreds of stories about the Carolinas, but no one ever mentions the searing heat. It's so hot that in the afternoon, no one and nothing moves. Work starts at 5:30 a.m. and ends at noon. Nobody works on a suntan here. They work at trying to avoid sunstroke. Even a diaper is too much clothing, if you know what I mean. Afternoons are spent lying under a shade tree or rocking on a shady porch.

The lady of the house, Cornellius, became Mrs. Bryant nine years ago. Cornellius is thirty-two years old, but she looks much younger than her years. In the cool of the morning, she will be picking fruit and flowers in the yard. She has a refreshing appearance in her sundress and straw hat. Her warm smile, sparkling eyes, and soft voice attract her neighbors, who join her for some early-morning socializing. She truly enjoys running the Bryant house.

Cornellius is happy because she now has the daughter she always wanted. Their five-year-old son, Jay Van, is in school, which leaves her days free to fill with her new baby. She dresses Cynthia in pretty dresses, rocks her in her favorite rocking chair, or carries her through the flower gardens.

She is a happy, fun, loving little girl who loves to play. On any given day, there are three or four kids playing in the Bryant yard. Cornellius—in her patient, kind manner—prepares them for school. Then, she rewards them with specially prepared treats. Before they know it, it is time for Cynthia to start school. She loves and enjoys the extended learning experience. All is well at the Bryant house.

Just after Cynthia's sixth birthday, Cornellius starts to have pain in her left arm. A visit to the family doctor reveals that she has arthritis. Her condition worsens steadily. Less than a year later, she has lost total use of her arm, and she is in constant pain. Cynthia helps her mom in the kitchen. She takes the ingredients out of the pantry or puts things away for her. She enjoys helping her mother pick flowers or fruit from the yard. These are happy times for Cynthia, spending summer days with her mom or playing with her friends.

Cynthia's best friend is her cousin Leroy. Leroy is ten years old and is like a big brother to her. He walks her to school and to church. They play together every day. He teaches her to ride a horse, catch fish, and climb trees. He loves to play tricks on the girls but protects them from the pranks of other boys. Beautiful horse-drawn carriages are the elite form of transportation. The Bryants have two horses, a carriage, and an old mule they call Sue. Leroy would sit Cynthia up on Sue and walk them deep into the woods to his favorite fishing hole. They think Sue is their pet when, in reality, her purpose is to till the large fields behind the barn, where Beerman plants his gardens.

By the time Cynthia turns eight years old, her mother, Cornellius, is bedridden. The arthritis has spread to her back and legs. In the summer of 1915, she dies due to complications of pneumonia. This is the most horrific experience for this little girl. Try as she does, she never recovers from the loss of her mother. She refuses to speak on the days that followed.

Beerman hires someone to cook and clean for his family, and Cynthia's favorite aunt comes to live with them. She goes with her father on summer days as he delivers the mail, or shops downtown. She helps him with the flowers and trees. She learns when and how to grow flowers, fruits, and vegetables. They even learn to bake cookies. In the evening, they sit on the porch, rocking as Beerman shares their family history with his daughter.

Due to health problems, Beerman retires early, giving them more time to share doing the things they enjoy. Summer turns to fall, and school days are back. As always, Leroy is waiting at the gate, ready to walk Cynthia; her best friend, Margaret; and their playmates to school.

At twelve years of age, she is a strong tall girl with clear skin, large dark eyes, and her mother's smile. Her greatest attributes are her abilities to listen and feel the true emotions of others. As fall moves toward winter, Beerman grows weaker. Within a few weeks, he joins Cornellius in eternal rest.

The weeks that followed Beerman's death are by far the hardest in Cynthia's life. At age thirteen, she is totally alone. Now, eighteen Jay Van is working and is seldom at home. As head of the household, Jay Van sells the house and all its contents. As a result, she loses all that connects her to her parents and everything that is personally hers. Life will never be the same for this little girl. She is sent to live with her uncle Major, aunt Cola, and their daughter May. Major and his family are cotton farmers. They live out in the country. Though she lost both parents, home, and everything that was a part of her life, no one and nothing can ever steal her memories—memories of her mother's love, her teachings, and her forgiving nature. Her love for and her devoted faith in God will live within her to sustain her in times that look darker than a country night. Major and Cola are the opposite of her parents. They are cold and distant, with razor-sharp tongues. Their eighteen-year-old daughter is mentally challenged, so they hide her out in the country with her problem. Because their daughter has problems with school, they keep her at home to work on the farm. May is not an attractive eighteen-year-old girl. No one has taken the time to teach her the things young girls are eager to learn. She has no interest in clothing, grooming, or socializing.

In the beginning, they see Cynthia as a means to attract young men to their house. Once she accomplishes this, she is expected to persuade them to date May. After a few of her friends become offended by her attempted matchmaking, she refuses to invite young men to Major's house. Her attitude brings out the wrath in Uncle Major, who now wants her to work in his fields, picking cotton. When she continuously passes out due to the extreme heat, Uncle Major concludes that she thinks she is too good to pick cotton. From this point on, everything that goes wrong, doesn't get done, or breaks is her fault. Imagine that this is you or your daughter alone in the world, living on the edge of nowhere with this dysfunctional family.

Because she cannot work in the fields, she has to wash, iron, cook, and clean for this family. Aunt Cola, being Major's wife, will not allow Cynthia to use her sewing kit or her oven. They give their daughter an allowance to purchase personal items when they go into town to shop. Because Cynthia can't work in the fields, they refuse to give her money for the things she needs. For two years, she meets her needs with the eighteen dollars that she receives from her brother. When she turns sixteen, Uncle Major decides school is not important as she is needed to help on the farm. After losing all, now she is being forced to quit school too. Personally, it seems, their daughter is not alone in her condition.

Now, nearly seventeen, Cynthia knows it is time for change. What faith and wisdom it must have taken her to leave this known hell for what might be worse. She knows that when she leaves, there can be no coming back. This Saturday, she is going to shop for a home. While in town, she speaks with Mrs. Paige. Mrs. Paige is the school librarian who knew Cornellius and Beerman even before Cynthia is born. Mrs. Paige, after losing her husband that year and now working a full-time job, struggles raising her six-year-old son. They agree Cynthia will cook and care for little Corey Monday through Friday. Mrs. Paige has a three-room cottage a short distance from her house that she agrees to rent to her. That afternoon, Cynthia meets with her best friend, Margaret, who is looking to move closer to her job but cannot afford to do it alone. Margaret jumps at the chance to be reunited with her lifelong friend. That night, Cynthia goes back to the farm, packs her belongings, and prepares for her final night on Major's farm. I'm sure she cannot sleep much this night. It is Sunday morning, and breakfast is over. Major and his family are sitting on the porch. She dresses for church, and then, she checks to make sure she hasn't left anything behind. She packs a fresh dip of snuff between her tongue and cheek, picks up her bags, and starts for the door for the last time. Looking at them sitting there on the porch, she thanks God for the past and steps off the porch into the future. Major's tongue is just as sharp this morning as it has always been; but this morning, it cuts a new path that leads to a better place—a place of her own.

Cynthia and Margaret work on their cottage all days of that week, and by Saturday, it is home. This Sunday morning, they have their first breakfast in their new home. This will be the first time these childhood friends go to church as children no more. As always when they are together, they laugh and talk as they dress for Sunday church services. On this afternoon, they decide to go to the church picnic. It is at this picnic that Margaret introduces Cynthia to Olen. Olen's family and Margaret's family have been neighbors and friends since before their children are born. Olen is eighteen years old, handsome, and has unusual eyes. He plays center field for the Clover Stars baseball team. He is the team's best player, which makes him popular with the young girls. The Sunday games are a family affair in Clover. People come from miles away to root for their favorite team. This Sunday, Olen hits two home runs, a triple and a double, which help the Clover Stars defeat the Rock Hill Tigers. When the game is over, Olen walks Cynthia and Margaret back to their cottage. They sit on the porch, laughing and talking, until Olen asks them to walk with him to speak to Aunt Pearla, who lives in the next cottage. When they reach Aunt Pearla's porch, they recognize her as a church elder and friend of their families. Though small in stature, she is strong in faith and wise even beyond her years. Aunt Pearla is eighty years old and totally blind, yet she lives alone. She has a daughter named Bessie who doesn't visit often, cook hot meals, do laundry, or clean her mother's house. In the days that followed, Cynthia visits Aunt Pearla almost daily. When she notices Bessie is not caring for Aunt Pearla, she shares her concerns with Mrs. Paige, who agrees. Mrs. Paige asks Cynthia to prepare a plate for Aunt Pearla each time she prepares a meal for her family. Mrs. Paige asks her to take the food to her and wait with her until she finishes her meal. She instructs her to dispose of the cold, sometimes-sour leftovers that her daughter leaves for her mother. Cynthia washes the dishes, cleans Aunt Pearla's house, and gathers her laundry as Aunt Pearla eats her meals. In the evening, she will go over to Aunt Pearla's house to wash and comb her hair or iron clothes for her to wear.

Months later, Aunt Pearla's daughter, Bessie, decides to move her family out in the country. Though she doesn't want to take her mother with her, she says she has no choice because Aunt Pearla cannot take care of herself. One morning, when Cynthia takes Aunt Pearla her breakfast, she finds her sitting in her room crying. She tells Cynthia of her daughter's plans to move and take her with her to the country. Cynthia does her best to calm Aunt Pearla's fears by assuring her that she will find a way to help her stay in her own home with people who love and care for her. On this occasion, she leaves Aunt Pearla eating breakfast on her front porch to go talk with Mrs. Paige.

It must have seemed like miles those twenty or thirty feet that separate that cottage and the main house where Mrs. Paige sits, sipping her morning coffee. She tells Mrs. Paige of Bessie's plan to move and take Aunt Pearla with her. When Cynthia tells Mrs. Paige that she found Aunt Pearla crying, Mrs. Paige becomes so upset a tear falls and splashes in her coffee cup.

Without looking up, she asks, "Are you willing to continue doing the things you have been doing for Aunt Pearla?" Cynthia smiles and then agrees, and a plan is born. Mrs. Paige, in her anger, utters, "The only way that booger Bess is going to take Aunt Pearla anywhere is over my dead body."

Anxious to share the news, Cynthia rushes back to Aunt Pearla's cottage. Her running confuses Aunt Pearla, who always recognizes her steps. She calls out, "Cynthia, is that you?"

A bit out of breath, she replies, "Yes, it's me, and Mrs. Paige is going to talk to Bessie about letting you stay here with us."

Aunt Pearla grabs her cane, stands up, and says, "Lord, *please* bless this child"; and it is done. That evening, Mrs. Paige is sitting on her porch so as not to miss Bessie when she walks past going to her mother's house. As the sun is slipping out of sight behind the trees, Bessie starts up the path that leads to Mrs. Paige's house. As Bessie approaches, Mrs. Paige beckons her to come up on the porch because she needs to speak with her. Heaven only knows what Mrs. Paige says to Bessie that day. Empty-handed Bessie walks to her mother's porch, where she stands for their conversation. A few minutes later, she turns and starts to walk away. Cynthia, sitting on her porch, recalls that it was a beautiful sound to hear Aunt Pearla say, "Bess, I hope you and your family enjoy that country, you hear?" Without so much as a wave, Bess moves out of sight down the walk.

Cynthia and Olen continue to date for almost two years. This Sunday is Aunt Pearla's eighty-third birthday. After church and the Sunday Stars game, Olen walks Cynthia and Margaret home. They go directly to Aunt Pearla's house to wish her a happy birthday. She wants to hear all about church and the outcome of the ball game. She asks Olen if he played better in her absence. As they sit talking, Olen says, "Old wise one, I'd like to ask you a question."

She barks back, "Boy, that's the only way you're going to get an answer."

"Do you think Cynthia might consider marrying me?"

She smiles, then, in her straightforward manner, replies, "Boy, you won't ever get married if you keep asking me. But since you are asking me, Cynthia is a nice young lady. She has no parents, so you will have to treat her right. If you think you are ready to do that, then you should ask her." Olen, still wearing his Stars baseball uniform, gets down on one knee before Cynthia and proposes.

Aunt Pearla gives them her blessing, laughs, and tells Olen, "I can see right now that I have to teach you everything, and I will." Cynthia and Margaret laugh, then cry, then laugh some more. They have a celebrating good time on this Sunday.

They find a small house just up the road from the cottage that she calls home. They spend evenings and weekends working on their new home. Olen moves into the house some months before the wedding because it is closer to his job. Six months later, on a Saturday afternoon, they are married. Of course, Margaret and Aunt Pearla are witnesses and honored guests.

It is August of 1927. Today, Cynthia learns that she is going to have her first child. On May 28, 1928, she gives birth to a daughter they call Lorraine. She spends the first two weeks at home with her new baby. When she goes back to work, she takes her baby with her. Lorraine spends many days on the porch with Aunt Pearla and Corey. Aunt Pearla enjoys these times, baby-sitting Lorraine and telling Corey stories. In between meals, Cynthia joins them to feed and spend time with Lorraine.

Moving On Up

It is 1929, and change is coming to the South. The machine age has arrived. This new era decreases the number of laborers on farms and in the mills so drastically that unemployment skyrockets. Men are forced to go miles away from their families to find work. Olen, having a new wife and baby, needs a full-time, permanent job. As time goes on, things only become worse. Earlier this year, Olen's friend Curtis Long goes up north to visit his brother. He writes Olen a letter telling him he found a job at a brickmaking company that is expanding and hiring. One week later, Olen is on a train, making the three-day trip to upstate New York. Within days upon his arrival, Olen has a job. He writes home and shares the news with his family. In less than a month, he finds a house and prepares for the day they will be able to join him. He furnishes the house and saves for their trip by taking on odd jobs in the evenings and on weekends.

A few months later, all is ready for their trip. Olen sends money for tickets and expenses, and then, he waits for them to arrive. Remember, this is 1929. Imagine train travel in these times. There is no air-conditioning, little if any heat, and no plush quarters. Now, this young woman is traveling more than a thousand miles with a nine-month-old baby. When does she sleep? Is there ever one moment free of fear? She has not been out of the South before. She has no idea what is front of her or what upstate New York holds. Even in her imaginative mind, she cannot imagine two feet of snow or temperatures of zero or below. With each hour, that train moves her closer and closer to her destiny. I wonder what she thinks of New York City as the train approaches and then enters it. She has to take all of her belongings and her baby from one train station to another in order to catch yet another train for the final four-hour ride to Kingston, New York. Three long days and even longer nights must seem like an eternity for her. Just the freedom to walk around would be a blessing in itself.

It has been almost four months since Olen left Clover and Lorraine was only four months old. Cynthia and Lorraine arrive in Kingston just after noon on Tuesday. When she steps off that train, Olen is there waiting. She says, "Now you are a sight for sore eyes." Their new home is nine miles north of Kingston. Olen borrows his friend Curtis's car to drive them home. Though small, the best description for home is "God's country." A river, mountains, trees, fields of grass and corn surround the fourteen or fifteen houses. All the land for miles belongs to the owner of a large brickyard located on the banks of the Hudson River. The bricks made at this yard are transported by boat to companies all over the state and beyond.

When she arrives, eight families from the Carolinas have already made that trip and now call this place home. In the morning after their men go off to work, the women get together to share news from family and friends back home. This networking of information makes friends of these new neighbors, who gain strength from each other and give support to whoever is in crisis.

The Seeds of Life

I'm still here in Cynthia's future genetic pool. I notice that there are four other special genes living here, which are destined to join Olen and Cynthia at different times in their future. Lorraine left the pool back in 1927 and is now their only child. She is four years old and the light of their lives.

As busy as a queen bee, Cynthia adds her personal touch to the four-bedroom house that Olen has selected to be their first home. This house is about to get dressed up home style. Room by room, Cynthia repaints every inch of the two-story wood frame house in shades of white. She then adds area rugs, curtains, small tables, an overstuffed chair, and lamps. Before long, nicknacks, plants, candles, and pictures take their place in her plan. A new soft lace tablecloth that looks tailor-made graces the dining room table. A floral piece, which she arranges with various cut flowers, adds color and beauty to the table. Through the screened windows, the sweet smell of lilac floats on a summer breeze, weaving its way from room to room. From the kitchen, located at the head of the stairs, cinnamon, apples baking, and fresh nutmeg announce the presence of fresh, out-of-the-oven apple pie. Pleased with her progress on the inside of the house, Cynthia makes a few additions to the area around the entrance to the house. Two large pots filled with blooming geraniums and a mix of wildflowers she planted in early spring add new life to the once-empty, colorless space. To complete this picture, she adds a new Welcome mat at the front door. The once-plain house located at Seventy-one Gray Fox Lane is now ready to house a family.

Summer has moved from upstate New York, and winter arrives. Olen, Cynthia, and Lorraine have been here for almost three years. For the past few weeks, Cynthia has not been her usual energetic self. Olen is concerned and suggests almost daily that she should visit Dr. Gifford for a checkup. Today, she is taking his advice. She takes a bus to nearby

Saugerties, New York. She walks the block or so to the doctor's office and arrives just in time for her appointment. She opens the door; enters the vestibule; and removes her boots, coat, and hat before proceeding to the receptionist. The woman wearing a white nurse's uniform and a warm smile greets her, saying, "You must be Cynthia because the doctor has only one patient this morning. My name is Anne Cambelle, and I'm Dr. Gifford's nurse and receptionist. The doctor will be with you shortly." Without missing a beat, the two start a conversation about the snow, then children. When Cynthia remarks about the headline on the sports page of the *Daily News*, they learn that they are both avid Brooklyn Dodgers fans. They spend the next ten minutes discussing their love for major league baseball. As they are beginning yet another topic, the door to the doctor's office opens, and Dr. Gifford joins them in the outer office. Anne stops talking long enough to introduce Cynthia to the doctor and to give him her chart. Dr. Gifford is a comforting spirit who makes everyone feel safe and at ease in his presence. After a physical exam and background questions, he assures Cynthia that in time, she will be her old self again. He stands up from his stool to walk over to his medicine cabinet. He takes a large bottle filled with pills from the cabinet and places it on the counter. He fills a small manila envelope with pills from the jar; then, he hands the envelope to Cynthia. He instructs her to take one of the pills each morning. He tells her that the pills are vitamins and that every expecting mother needs additional vitamins during her pregnancy. He tells her to make an appointment to see him again in eight weeks. Cynthia has not said a word since the doctor mentioned the word *pregnancy*. When she finds her voice, she asks the doctor if he is sure of his prediction. Next, she inquires when the baby will arrive. As she walks to the door of his office, Dr. Gifford remarks, "Yes, I'm sure, and you will be too by the time you come back to see me. Believe me, Cynthia, I am never wrong about such a thing. You will give birth in July of next year." He opens the door of his office and escorts Cynthia over to Anne's desk. He instructs Anne to make an appointment for Cynthia. He tells Anne that her new friend is going to be a new mom. Wearing a full smile on her face, Anne extends her hand to Cynthia and wishes her a healthy, happy journey. "If you have any doubt about the doctor's calculations, you can be rest assured that you are pregnant, and you will deliver in July. I've worked with the doctor for nine years. He is always right about these things."

It has been almost four years since Cynthia gave birth to Lorraine. She is surprised that she did not experience the symptoms she had with her first child. As she leaves the doctor's office and walks along Main

Street, she recalls experiencing morning sickness a few weeks back. Even before the bus ride home was over, she knows that Dr. Gifford is probably right. As she walks down the lane toward home, she wonders why. Even when she has been under the weather with a flu or a cold, Olen has never before suggested that she visit the doctor. She dismisses the thought, telling herself that he cannot know because she doesn't know herself. Her short walk down the lane ends at her front door. She puts her key in the door and enters the quiet, empty house. She removes her hat, coat, and her boots before proceeding upstairs to start dinner. Alone in her kitchen, she finally accepts the reality of her condition and wonders if this child she is carrying is a boy or a girl. For the first time since she learned of the new life within, she smiles at the prospect of a new addition to her family. Her thoughts are interrupted by the sound of the front door opening and Lorraine calling her from downstairs. She stops preparing the meal to walk to the head of the stairs to say hello to Lorraine, who continues calling up to her as her father removes her hat, snowsuit, and boots. When Lorraine can see her at the head of the stairs, she stops squirming and allows her father to remove her boots. Before the boots hit the floor, Lorraine is halfway up the stairs and already sharing the experiences of her afternoon with her father to her mother. Cynthia bends down, kisses her baby, and carries her into the kitchen. She places her on one of the kitchen chairs as she listens to the story of her sleigh ride and the snowball fight with her dad. As Lorraine continues, Cynthia makes hot chocolate to warm her little girl. Olen comes into the kitchen, and though they talk for some time, neither of them mentions her visit to the doctor.

Olen has not mentioned that just last week, he was the one experiencing nausea and the inability to keep food in his stomach. His buddies began teasing him after he became ill one morning. They informed Olen that when a man experiences such symptoms, it is a sign that his mate is carrying his child. The next time the guys noticed that Olen was again not feeling well, they were sure that he is, indeed, going to be a father. They are now *beyond* wondering if he is going to be a father; they are betting on whether the child Cynthia carries is a boy or a girl. Somewhere in the midst of dinner, Olen inquires about the results of Cynthia's visit with the doctor. Cynthia lifts her head, looks across the table, and places her gaze on Olen. In silence, she waits for his eyes to meet hers before she proceeds to answer. When she has his undivided attention, she shares the secret that has been on the tip of her tongue and in her mind for hours. "The good doctor says that we are going to be a family of four this next July. It has taken me hours to adjust, accept, and enjoy the thought of becoming a mother again." As though totally relieved, she awaits his response. When Olen first inquired, his expression was one of somber concern. When he learns that the news is all good, his expression goes from a slick grin to a full smile of surprise and contentment. Knowing all is well in paradise, Olen lets loose with a barrage of questions.

He begins by saying, "You mean you went off to the doctor with a cold and come home a mother-to-be? Are you sure? When is the baby expected to arrive?" Bearing witness to Olen's immediate pleasure, Cynthia explains that Dr. Gifford is sure that she is pregnant and that the baby will arrive in July of next year. Excited at the prospect of fatherhood and relieved that his sympathy pains will subside, Olen shares his joy first with the guys and then everyone else that he encounters for the next few weeks.

In the weeks and months that followed, Cynthia goes through every phase that precedes delivery. She gains weight, retains fluids; yet she smiles a lot. Her skin takes on a new glow; her hair and nails seem to grow overnight. She takes long walks each morning and short naps in the afternoon. She craves for chocolate candy and ice cream. Her back hurts, her ankles swell, and she hasn't seen her feet in weeks. She is now ready to get on with the delivery phase. On this cloudy Saturday in mid-July, as Olen pulls weeds from her flower beds and Lorraine picks wildflowers and weeds, the time for change comes. While standing in front of Lorraine's dresser, selecting socks to match the outfit she has chosen for Lorraine to wear in the coming days, she receives the first sign.

Just moments ago, Cynthia was uncomfortable, but free of pain. It's late morning when the first contraction attracts her attention. In preparation for her hospital stay, she adds the final items to her bag. Over the next three to four hours, the frequency and duration of pain increases steadily. By late afternoon, the contractions are frequent and strong enough to make the decision to leave for the hospital a wise one. From the bedroom window, she asks Olen to bring Lorraine upstairs. When they enter the bedroom, she tells Lorraine that if she promises to be a good girl, she can go play with the kids next door. Cynthia gives her baby a kiss; then, she straightens her yellow bows and sends her off to play. As Lorraine skips across the room toward the door, Cynthia tells Olen that it's time to leave for the hospital. In that lean-back fashion that becomes a part of the appearance of soon-to-be moms, she starts the trip toward motherhood. After a slow and deliberate sequence of short steps, she reaches the car. Much maneuvering is required to find a way to get into the car that doesn't cause the onset of yet another contraction.

Olen drives the short distance to where Lorraine is playing with Ida's five-year-old daughter. Ida, seeing her friend Cynthia with the overnight bag, knows that the time has come. Ida has already agreed to care for Lorraine while Olen drives Cynthia to the hospital. Through the open car window, Cynthia gives her friend a wave, which means that there is no time to continue this conversation. Cynthia knows that both Dr. Gifford and nurse Cambelle will be at the hospital when they arrive.

As Olen heads the car up the long driveway that leads to the hospital's entrance, they see nurse Cambelle standing on the open porch, talking to one of her patients. She walks across the porch, then down the stairs, and over to the passenger side of the car. She smiles at Cynthia then imparts her calming humor. "Gee, Cynthia, on such a lovely day, I thought you might be in Brooklyn rooting for the Dodgers. Let's see if we can't make it possible for you to attend next Sunday's game." Olen and Anne assist Cynthia out of the car and into the hospital.

Over the next four to five hours, Cynthia's contractions peak, ebb, then peak again. The contractions become more intense. When they have accomplished their purpose, life wins the battle. With one final push, the crown of Cynthia's little prince appears. Within minutes, Dr. Gifford is holding a screaming baby boy in his hands. He carries the baby up from the foot of the bed along the side so that Cynthia can see and touch her first son. Dr. Gifford gives Cynthia a pat on her arm as he says, "Well, Cynthia, it's Sunday, July 10; and we have this brand-new baby boy. My work is done here. I must examine, weigh, and clean this little fella up as his dad is waiting." The doctor carries the child from the room, but Anne remains to assist Cynthia. A short time later, Dr. Gifford returns, telling Cynthia that he has shared the news of her new son with Olen. A few minutes later, Anne steps out into the waiting room to tell Olen that he can now see his wife. Anne joins Dr. Gifford to prepare this newborn for their first family gathering. When Anne completes her pampering of the muscular little man child with a full head of hair and ebony eyes, she wraps him in a blue receiving blanket. Anne smiles at the thought of delivering this bundle of joy to her new friend. Her smile is still evident as she enters Cynthia's room. Because Cynthia has seen their child before, Anne places the little prince in his father's arms. After a moment of adjusting to the small, little warm bundle that can be held in his hands, Olen lifts the blanket away from the head and face of the infant. Wearing a whisper of a smile on his face, Olen tries to take in everything about the baby. His full head of hair, his tiny fingers, his lip sucking, and his every move are noted. Finally, almost in a whisper, Olen speaks to his child, saying, "Well, little man, I think you are hungry; so you need to be with your mother now." The picture of Olen watching Cynthia feed their first son brings a smile of approval to Anne's face as she leaves the room. On Sunday, Olen and Cynthia decide to name their son Robert in remembrance of Olen's brother who gave his life in the war. After a week with Dr. Gifford and Anne, it is time to return home and enjoy the experience of raising Robert.

When summer ends, Lorraine is off to kindergarten. The months turn into years. Each day, it seems Robert learns something to let them know that soon it will be his turn to start school. He is already riding a tricycle, reciting his *ABCs*, and trying to run with the big boys. Things have a way of repeating themselves just to make sure that no one forgets the past. It's been three years since Robert became their number one son. Olen has taken Robert for a haircut, which leaves Cynthia free to visit with her friend Anne. As they catch up on everything from flowers to baseball, Dr. Gifford opens the door of his office to say hello. Dr. Gifford tells Cynthia that it's been awhile since she last stopped in to see them. Cynthia knows this is the time to get the good doctor's opinion or confirmation. "Well, I really stopped by for some of your vitamins, that is, if you have any left," she states.

The doctor beckons her into his office, saying, "If what you say is true, you know that I have vitamins just for you."

Friday night is family night for Olen, Cynthia, and the kids. They always drive the nine miles to Kingston to shop, to eat dinner, and to visit. Olen and Robert go to the barbershop or to the Elks Club while Cynthia and Lorraine shop. They meet for dinner before they visit Cynthia's brother, Jay Van; his wife, Margaret; and their son, Willie.

On this Friday, Olen and Robert return just after Cynthia completes her personal errands and grocery shopping. Olen places her shopping bags in the trunk; then he parks the car in the parking lot. They always walk the block or so to Fair Street's busy district. There are clothing stores, a toy store, jewelry store, drugstore, soft ice cream shop, and a second-hand store on the first block of Fair Street. Cynthia's favorite shop is Olsen's Priceless Pieces. Olsen's is a second-hand store that always has unique pieces in the window. Mr. Olsen is from Savannah, Georgia. They say he goes on buying trips all through the South. This accounts for the various styles of furniture in his shop.

As Cynthia approaches Olsen's window, she is frozen in place by the sight of a china closet. Olen and Robert are walking ahead and are not aware that Cynthia is three shops back and still standing in front of Olsen's shop. Looking over his shoulder, Olen notices that Cynthia is not behind them, but she is still looking into Olsen's window. She continues gazing into the window until Olen and Robert walk back to her side. She explains to Olen that she has not seen a china cabinet like the one in the window since she was a little girl. After some prompting from the kids, Cynthia joins in step with the family. Each Friday through that summer and fall, Cynthia, because of her continued fascination with this cabinet, would show the china closet to Olen. Later, Olen makes a special trip to Olsen's to venture into the shop for a closer look at this piece that has Cynthia mesmerized. A few weeks pass; when Cynthia and Olen are Christmas shopping for their kids, she is compelled to walk past Olsen's to look at the china cabinet. She looks, as always, into the window for her Friday look at the cabinet, reminiscing of her childhood; but she cannot believe that her favorite piece no longer occupies its place in Olsen's window. A look of quiet shock and disbelief blankets her sad face. Noticing the change, Olen asks, "What's the matter?" Then she replies that it's gone.

"What's gone?"

"My cabinet. It's not in the window."

As serious as he wants to be, Olen replies, "This is a business, not Olsen's home. Those things in there are for sale. That thing has been in that window for months. I'm sure he will have another one by next Friday." Olen turns away from the window and is ready to move on. When Cynthia doesn't join his steps, Olen asks, "Are we going to spend the night looking in an empty window?" I don't think she hears a word Olen is saying. Olen has no idea that the removal of that cabinet from Olsen's window will affect Cynthia in such a way. Taking her hand, he urges his wife's steps beyond the store window. Cynthia is no longer in the mood for Christmas shopping, and she simply wishes to go home.

With four days left until Christmas, Cynthia and her friend Ida need to finish their shopping. This time, Ida's husband, Herb, joins them. Herb works at the brickyard with Olen and is Olen's hunting and fishing partner. As always, leaving the guys time to fill with whatever they like, the ladies go off to shop. Today, Olen and Herb have two hours to get to Olsen's and load that china closet on the top of Olen's car, drive it to Herb's house, and then get back to meet their wives. Ida and Herb have heard about the china cabinet and are now part of keeping the secret from Cynthia.

With all the decorations in place and gifts wrapped and under the tree, seven-year-old Lorraine and almost-four-year-old Robert are having trouble getting to sleep. Cynthia is almost three months into her third pregnancy, and the events of the day are going to make sleep come easy for her. Long before the sun rises over this quiet country setting, kids who can't wait another minute will be opening those perfectly wrapped presents. Somewhere around 6:30 a.m., Robert and Lorraine awaken Cynthia and Olen and are ready to see what Santa Claus left them. Olen has been awake for more than an hour. Olen is just a big kid where Christmas is concerned. Robert receives a sleigh and Lorraine the ice skates that she's been asking for almost daily. When all the presents have been opened and breakfast is over, it's time to try out that new sleigh and those skinny white skates. Cynthia helps the kids dress for sleigh riding and ice-skating. She places Robert on his new sleigh, pulls him next door, invites Ida and her eight-year-old daughter Sarah, and walks with them to the ice-skating pond. Sarah is jumping with joy since she too received skates from Santa. The skating pond is almost a half mile away from their homes. While the girls spend more time getting up off the ice than skating and Ida and Cynthia spend time pulling Robert on his sleigh, Olen and Herb were busy. As soon as their wives and children are out of sight, they carry the china cabinet from Ida and Herb's house next door to its new home in Cynthia's kitchen. Olen and Herb take Cynthia's cups and saucers from their place on the shelf and place them inside the china cabinet.

Herb and Ida have three sons and two daughters. They are all outside and enjoying making a snowman and having a snowball fight. The boys get their sleighs, and they all head off to the ice-skating pond. The boys show Robert how to use his sleigh on the small hills near the pond. The girls skate until their fingers and toes grow numb. Olen then suggests that they all return to the house for something hot to drink and a slice of Cynthia's apple pie.

Happy, cold, and hungry for sweet treats, they sing Christmas carols on the walk home. Once inside, the older kids help the younger ones with their boots before they head upstairs. Ida waits as Cynthia changes Robert's wet clothes and socks. Due to the number of people in what usually seems like a large room, Olen; Herb; and Herb's eldest son, Leo, are standing shoulder to shoulder at one side of the room. Ida takes Robert's hand and allows him to lead the way upstairs. Ida follows Robert, making certain that Cynthia is the last to enter her kitchen. Olen tells Cynthia that they have hot water for tea, coffee, and hot chocolate. He explains that they cannot find her cups and saucers. Cynthia instinctively turns to the shelf where she has always kept the cups and saucers. While Cynthia has her back turned, Olen, Herb, and Leo step away from the front of the cabinet. Olen then says, "Why don't we use these cups and saucers?" When Cynthia turns around, Olen is pointing to her cups and saucers that are now inside the china cabinet that she admired in Olsen's window.

Cynthia cannot believe her eyes. She is taken back to a time when she was a little girl. She covers her eyes with her hands. Peeking through her fingers, as children do when playing hide-and-seek, she makes sure that her eyes are not playing tricks on her. A scream of joy slips from her lips as tears slide down her cheeks. She first gives Olen a kiss and a hug, and then she whispers something in his ear. Cynthia touches, hugs, or kisses each and everyone in her kitchen. She thanks Olen for bringing a piece of her old home to their new home on Gray Fox Lane. I have not seen Cynthia this excited or happy since she was a very little girl. Holding Olen's hand in her hands as though doing so would keep her feet planted on the floor, she takes a few steps to where this piece from her past now resides. As though alone with her memories, Cynthia inspects the cabinet first with her eyes, then through her sense of touch. She inspects the grain of the wood, the color, and the unforgettable smell inside the glass door. She knows that everyone in her kitchen is warm and satisfied because every cup is empty and every plate is clean. Still touching the cabinet, she confesses that it is a true likeness to the one her parents owned when she was a child. Without interruption to her inspection, she thanks Olen and everyone who helped make this Christmas extra special. Many things come and go from the house, but that china cabinet still occupies its special place in any place that they call home.

It's one of those summer Sundays at the end of May, as flowers bloom and temperatures rise, that another special gene starts its trip to life. Church and dinner are in the past. The only sound coming from the kitchen is the sound of the radio announcer giving a play-by-play description of the Sunday's Dodgers baseball game. Though this has been the easiest of her pregnancies, Cynthia still takes her afternoon naps. But first, she looks out the kitchen window down at the kids who are playing pitch and catch, jumping rope, and horseshoes. Olen and Herb are tinkering with one of the many projects. This is a good time for a nap. The sound of the kids playing and the game on the radio serenade Cynthia into restful sleep. When she awakens, the kids are still playing, and the game is far from over. Sitting on the side of the bed with one hand on her stomach, she can feel this child moving. Contractions for this child are mild, brief, yet frequent. The movement continues. It's as though he or she is repositioning himself or herself. First, there is a kick from a foot or a knee, followed by total inactivity. Looking down, she watches as it changes the shape of her stomach as her unborn baby slips lower and lower into a place of comfort. This time, it's not about pain and hours of contractions. It has been less than thirty minutes, and this child travels farther than any of the previous babies had moved in four to six hours. At this rate, this baby might deliver himself or herself right here at home. Ida comes upstairs to check on Cynthia. As they discuss the rapid descent into the birth canal of this child, it continues its downward progression. Ida walks over to the window and yells down. "Olen, it's time to hitch up the horses and ride," she says. Her tone tells him it's time to bring the car, get the bag, and be off. Cynthia and Ida laugh, saying, "At this rate, this child could be here before sunset." They will laugh about that for years. Less than forty-five minutes after Cynthia enters the delivery room at Dales Hospital, her second son, Albert, slides into Dr. Gifford's hands. All of Cynthia's babies have been a cross between Olen, Cynthia, and their families. Albert is exclusively Cynthia's son, as he looks identical to her in every way. As he grows, he becomes even more like her. He is quiet, peaceful, strong, tall, and always aims to please. Learning comes easy for him. He is the only one of her children who learns music. He loves the drums, trumpet, and sax.

Much has changed over the past ten years at Seventy-one Gray Fox Lane and in Glasco. The addition of two boys seems to fill every free moment in Cynthia's life. This little hamlet called Glasco is experiencing a population explosion too. The fifty-seven children born here over the past ten years created a need for an addition to the existing grade school.

It's 1938; Cynthia and Lorraine are outnumbered in this house of little men and Olen. Albert is four years old, and he follows Robert and Olen everywhere they go. While they are out and about, Cynthia and Lorraine experiment with a new hairstyle. Now eleven years old, Lorraine feels that pigtails are for little girls. Somewhere in their conversation, Cynthia remarks that they need another girl in this house. Lorraine remarks, "Let's make the next baby a girl, Mom," and it was done. On April 5 of the following year, Ruby came into and took over the hearts of everyone. She is a beautiful baby. Though she looks more like Olen, she has her mother's ways.

There are now only two special genetic seeds remaining here in the pool, and one of them is preparing to join in the light of life.

THE FIFTH SEED

Cynthia and Olen are both thirty-seven years old, and they have two boys and two girls. They couldn't be happier, or so they thought. Back in December, old doctor Gifford, who is never wrong, confirms her suspicions. He says that she should give birth again in mid-June. She shares the news with Olen and the kids, and time marches on.

Seasons change like the night; it's 8:27 a.m., June 15, when Cynthia's contractions are *fifteen minutes apart*. She informs Olen that today is the day. He dismisses her prediction, pulls the covers over his head, and takes a nap. At 10:45 a.m., she awakens him saying that the contractions are *ten minutes apart*. Olen is a calm man with discipline and direction. Something about the word *contractions* has rattled him. He jumps up, still half asleep. He stumbles over the overnight bag. Then, he has trouble putting his clothes on. He spends five minutes walking back and forth looking for his keys, which are exactly where they always are. He grabs his keys and cap, and he runs down the stairs. In his haste, he has forgotten the overnight bag and the main reason for this unscheduled trip: Cynthia. Somewhere between the house and the garage, he remembers his wife and soon mother-to-be. One would think this is the first time he has been through this experience. He is back in the house, telling Cynthia she should hurry. She makes a big mistake in telling him that the contractions are *eight minutes apart*. Finally, she helps him to the car, which is still in the garage. To save time, he opens the garage door, and they get into the car.

Olen loves his new Oldsmobile that he always drives with great care. On this occasion, there is someone else sitting in the driver's seat. This guy is possessed! He starts the engine, puts the car in reverse, and hits the accelerator all in one motion. We are out of the garage at forty miles per hour. At this rate, a hospital might not be necessary! Well, the contractions are *six minutes apart*. His erratic driving makes her nervous.

I don't know what *nervous* is, but I don't like it either. I'm no policeman, but sixty in a forty-miles-per-hour zone is overspeeding.

We arrive or land at the hospital, and a new ride begins. Now, we have a new driver behind the wheelchair. I think Olen must have taught this psycho all he knows about driving. Where are those Baby Onboard signs when you need one? Finally, we are out of that two-wheel suicide vehicle. Cynthia is up on the table in a rare position. The doctor is asking strange questions, like he wants to know if her water has broken. How do you break water? He says, "It's going to be a C-section delivery."

Well, hold on! We were off again; now, we're on a flying table. Thank God, there isn't much traffic in these halls. Now that we are in the operating room, the doctor says, "It's showtime!" I don't have lights in here, so therefore, I can't see what they are doing. But Cynthia is out. With all that is going on, I really can't talk now. I will see you later.

By the way, did I tell you it's my time to see the light? My estimated time of arrival (ETA) is any minute now.

It's 11:45 a.m. Friday, June 15—this day dawned in a ray of sunshine, blanketed by blue skies. The crickets, roosters, and birds have completed their daily routines. It's almost noon, and the baddest mom on the planet is putting the finishing touches on my entry into this world. She deserves a break today! Because of my size and position, natural birth is not possible. My C-section entry is necessary so that both of us will survive the journey. It's noon, Friday, June 15—halfway through the day and halfway through the year. At last, I have arrived.

I am taken from my safe dark warm home in the womb and cleaned from head to toe by perfect strangers. They dress me. That is a first! They even put booties and a hat on me. They carry me to a room filled with little beds made just for babies. As this angel in white walks between the rows of little beds, I notice all the babies are crying. What could cause five babies to cry? Since I have always had a continuous food supply in my home in the womb, I have no idea that we are now at the mercy of angels for food. As she carries me past each baby, I notice they are all made the same. They don't have much hair, no teeth, and no real color. My angel comes to a place in the middle of that white room, and she places me in my very own little bed. She covers me with a blanket, and leaves. For the first time, I am alone.

Who am I? Where did I come from? Who do I belong to? I try to stay awake—really, I do. I have spent the last five hours on the trip of my life, and I am tired. I sleep until the angel comes to get me. She picks me up and, without a word, carries me to another part of the fourteen-bed hospital. She enters a small room with a single bed, nightstand, table, and chair. There are fresh flowers on the table and wildflowers in a vase on the windowsill.

In the sterile white bed is the most beautiful woman. She is totally different from anyone I'd yet meet. She has great color and large dark eyes. She is tall and strong, and she too looks as though she has taken the same tiring trip.

At the sight of Ann, the nurse carrying me, she smiles and extends her arms to receive me. This is my first smile. I decide smiles are good things. As Ann places me in the arms of this stranger, Cynthia says, "Thank you, Ann; she's beautiful!" These are the first words I ever heard, and I love the way they bounce around in my head. I notice something familiar as I lay my head on her shoulder. I recall hearing this voice many times when I lived in her womb. This is the woman who carried me. Ann leaves the room; and almost immediately, she takes me in her hands, holds me away from her, and she says, "Hello, baby, I'm your mom. My name is Cynthia. And because of all we have gone through, your name is Cynthia too. Your middle name is Ann after Ann Campbell, the nurse who just brought you to me. Our last name is Tate. We acquired that when I married your father. You will meet him later. He's at home with your two sisters and two brothers."

She has a clear, strong voice that touches your heart and warms your soul. She also has large brown eyes that almost smile when she is pleased. I hear every word she says, and I understand that I am special and important because I am a part of her. I want to repeat the word *mom* to her because when she says it to me, it makes her smile. And I want to see that smile again.

It is almost 4:00 p.m. now. Though I am safe and warm lying up against my mom's breasts, something is happening. I recall back in the operating room when they took me out of my mother's womb. We were connected. I am alive because she was my host. Just before I left that room, one of those angels dressed in white cut that cord, and we were one no more.

Now there is an irritating feeling in the pit of my stomach that won't go away. I know I can't talk but don't know another way to tell my mom about this pain. As the moments go by, I am becoming even more frustrated. Finally, I must let my mom know something is wrong. She positions me up on her shoulder and rubs my back. Um . . . that feels good, but my stomach still hurts. Finally, I get so angry that I try to talk again, but again, that doesn't work. Maybe I should try doing what the five babies were doing when I met them, so I cry! As my mom kisses me, I stop crying. She kisses me again. I recall kisses are good things! I like kisses, and I want more of them. But kisses don't stop the pain in my stomach, so I go back to making that awful, loud noise. This time, Mom leans back on her pillow, opens her robe, and places me inside next to her warm full breast. She takes her breast in hand and gently pushes her nipple in between my lips. Instinctively, I begin sucking on it. There is something all too familiar about the taste of Mother's milk. As I lie there enjoying my first feast, I hear the familiar sound of her heart beating next to my ear. I remember thinking that it can't get any better than this. The milk from Mom's breast has stopped the pain. I'm calm and satisfied. This seems like the perfect time and place for a nap.

I awaken a few hours later back in the nursery with my five new friends. I'm not feeling that pain in my stomach anymore. Now, there's something wrong with the bottom of my outfit. While I slept, someone wet my diaper. It's cold and wet, and no one seems to notice. There is so much water here that it's wetting my bed too. If I don't tell them I'm wet, I will have to lie in this wet place. Since crying worked when my stomach hurt, I'm going to do that again. After a few minutes of my screaming, Ann comes into the room. She looks over the room, follows the noise, and starts toward me. She leans over my bassinet and says, "So what's wrong, Cynthia?" She checks to see if I am wet; then, she goes across the room to the supply cart, comes back, and changes me and my bed. Again, I am happy.

It's now Saturday morning; Mom gives me a bath, feeds me, and dresses me. She's happy and excited as though someone special was coming. I become tired just before noon, and I have to take a nap. I awaken to people laughing and talking. They have come to see my five little friends. Ann, the resident angel, comes to take me to my mom. I always enjoy this part. Each time I go to her room, I receive something new or good. This trip is no exception because when we enter the room, my mother is not alone. Sitting in a chair next to her bed is a clean-shaven light-skinned man who looks like one continuous muscle. The nurse hands me to my mom, and after a brief conversation with the man in the chair, she leaves the room.

My mom is sitting on the side of her bed. She is facing the man in the chair. She pulls me to her, kisses me gently on the cheek, and smiles as she says, "Cynthia, this is your dad."

All in one motion, she sits me on his lap. Instinctively, he puts his hands around my shoulders and back. When I look up into his face, he almost smiles. As I look higher, I notice his eyes. They are the color of a field of wheat, and the wheat waves as though pushed by a gentle breeze. He has very sharp, distinctive features and a flawless complexion. We sit, checking each other out, until he says, "Do you know how long I've been waiting for you?" I can't talk, yet I know it isn't the right time to cry. I smile, and he gives me one in return. I'm happy I came here; I get to meet Mom and Dad. I receive smiles, hugs, and kisses. Right now, I'm almost colorless like the other babies. I hope someday soon to have a beautiful tan like my mother and a clear complexion like my father. It was great inside the womb, but out here is the place for me.

I hear Mommy and Daddy talking today. She says tomorrow is Sunday. My first Sunday! It sounds special. The kids, as they call them, are going to church Sunday morning. Dad says the church sisters are fixing lunch for them so that they don't have to go back home. Visiting hours start at one o'clock here, and they are coming to see Mom and meet me. Mom says I have two brothers and two sisters. I wonder what brothers and sisters are. Are they small like me or big like Mom and Dad? Do they have teeth, can they walk, or will Dad carry them?

I still can't talk, but I have questions, like "Why does that woman say that visiting hours are now over every night?" I never see her, but I hear her. Oh, by the way, this morning, a funny little guy came to see Mom and me. He is dressed in all white with a pin on his jacket that reads "Dr. Wilson." After talking to Mom, he takes me out of her arms and places me on the changing table. Since Mom doesn't object, I don't cry. First, the funny guy has cold hands, and then, there is that mirror in the middle of his forehead. We just met, and already, this guy is getting really close. He's looking in my eyes, nose, and ears; and now, he's in my mouth. Why is it that the people who can talk don't say anything and that those of us who can't talk have something to say, like, "Could you warm that stethoscope? It's giving me chills. Mom, Mom, are you watching this guy?" He's tickling my feet and pulling my arms! Oh! Oh! He's making faces. Now, he's making jokes about my hair. The way I see it, he needs more on the top. Oh no, now, he's taking my shirt off! Somebody tell this guy that I'm shy. What is he going to do next? Well, he's going to take my temperature, and he's not going for my mouth. I'm not happy, and I want my mom. So I'm going to cry. Thank God that works. I don't know what I would have done if he hadn't handed me back to my mom.

He tells Mom I'm healthy and strong, but she has to stay a few more days. Now, I'm upset, hungry, and tired. The funny man isn't funny anymore, and I'm glad he's gone. Mom gives me a smile and a kiss, and I stop crying. Now, she's feeding me my favorite stuff. I'm warm again. I've eaten, so you know what I'm going to do now? Sleep! Mom says Dad came to see us, but I slept through that. I'm trying to rest up for Sunday. So far, I've learned that Dad doesn't work on Saturdays or Sundays. The kids are with him on Sunday when they go to church. On this Sunday, ladies from their church prepare lunch for them before they come to see us. I like Sundays already.

It's still Saturday night; the nurse is taking me back to my mom's room. I wonder why. My dad just left! When we enter Mom's room, there is a pretty girl sitting on the bed next to my mom. She has big brown eyes with a nice tan like Mom's; she has sparkling white teeth and long arms and legs.

She's standing by the bed now. Although she is almost as tall as Mom, she's only sixteen. Ann seems to know her too. She says, "Lorraine, this is your little sister Cynthia. Would you like to hold her?" So this is a sister! I think I'm going to like sisters. She has long hair unlike mine. She puts me up against her breasts with my head on her shoulder. Her hair is soft, it smells good, and it tickles. She's rubbing my back. I like the way she lets me sit on her arm. She brushes my hair, and she talks to me too. So far, the only bad part of being a baby is not being able to talk. I'd like to tell my sister Lorraine that I think her name is almost as pretty as she is; but I can't talk yet. The very next time she puts me up on her shoulder, I'm going to kiss her like Mommy kisses me. Do you think big sisters like little baby kisses?

It must be Sunday. It's real early—barely daylight—and I'm still in bed with Mom. This morning, I don't have to cry to have my diaper changed. Mom changes me, bathes, and dresses me.

The sun is up now. Birds are singing outside the open window. Ann is putting fresh flowers in all the rooms. I am fascinated by their smell and color. All the other moms have their babies with them, so nobody is crying.

Mom says the doctor wants her to start walking around today. So we are going for a walk. At the other end of the hallway, there is a sunroom. It has many windows that are all opened this morning. This is my first time in the sunroom. It's really bright. That big yellow ball outside the window is warm, and it feels good. Outside, there are bushes with flowers on them like the ones in Mom's room. There is a big green blanket all around the front of the hospital. Two guys are spraying water on the flowers and on the blanket. Mom says they are watering the grass.

My mom is standing in front of an open window. She can see grown-ups and children coming toward us. It must be one o'clock because they are coming to visit my five little friends. There's a black shiny car coming up the driveway. Mom starts smiling at the sight of it. Ann smiles and says, "Cynthia, your family has arrived." It's from that window that I first see my sisters and my brothers. When the car comes to a stop, it is across the grass from the open window.

My father is the first to emerge from the car. He is handsome in his pressed gray suit, starched white shirt, and black shiny shoes. He is wearing a new straw hat. It's no wonder that I'm so cute! We are a three-flavor family. Dad is vanilla, Mom is chocolate, and I'm strawberry red.

From the passenger side of the car comes my sister Lorraine. Wearing a new dress and stockings and shiny shoes, she is sparkling clean and pressed. Both back doors open, and out of each door come the boys. They are my brothers, Robert and Albert. Robert is my older brother. Though only twelve years old, he already has a muscular build. Robert has on slacks, a white shirt, tie, shoes, and socks. Albert is now outside the other door. Albert is eight years old, and he looks like Mom. He's cute in his short pants and short-sleeve shirt. There's still someone left in the car. Finally, out pops a really cute little girl. She's almost five years old. Ruby is surely going to be a model. Oh, they can all walk! They have hair and teeth, and each one has his or her own degree of tan. Lorraine is walking in front of Dad; she's holding Ruby's hand. Robert and Albert are running up the walkway. Lorraine and Dad wave at us, and Mom waves back. Looking over my mom's shoulder, I can see the boys running down the hall toward us. They must really miss Mom because they haven't stopped running since they got out of the car. I can tell Mom is excited to see them too. Dad and Lorraine are coming down the hall. Robert gets to us first. He has a full face, nice curly hair, and a wide grin. As Robert stands close to Mom, she reaches down and touches his face as she says hello. He reaches into his pocket to hand her a four-leaf clover. She smiles, thanks him, and whispers something in his ear. Whatever she says makes him smile. Albert, the eight-year-old, is pulling on Mom's dress. She hands me to Dad; then she bends down to kiss my brother. Albert is a quiet, shy little boy with a head full of bad hair, but he does have nice legs for a boy.

Now that they have gotten their hugs and kisses, they are ready to go play. Lorraine has me sitting on her lap with my back resting against her breasts so that I can see everyone. Mom and Dad are standing by the open window in front of me. Lorraine kisses me on the top of my head; then, she tries to fix my hair with her fingers. When is she going to introduce me? Finally, Robert, my oldest brother, takes hold of one of my fingers and says, "Even though you're not a boy, we will keep you." I must remember that he likes to be called Bobby, not Robert. I give his finger a squeeze, and he lets me continue to hold on. I think Albert wants to touch me, but he's not ready now.

Ruby has been standing in front of me for five minutes, but she hasn't said a word. All at once, she steps back, spins around in a circle like models do, and says, "My name is Ruby, and this is my new dress and my

Sunday shoes." She comes over to me and, almost in a whisper, says, "Dad tells me that you can't talk, but you have a nice gummy little smile." Now, she's cracking on my gums. She's so cute that I think I'm going to let her get away with that one. She has the longest of eyelashes, a shy smile, and the cutest dress. Maybe one day, she will let me wear it.

In all the excitement, my diaper gets wet again. Lorraine tells Mom I need to be changed. Mom tells Lorraine that she can do it if she likes to. Ruby and Lorraine are taking me back to Mom's room for the change. My brothers are staying with Mom and Dad. It's funny that my little brother is almost as big as my big brother. Brothers are good, but sisters are the best! They change me and powder me and carry me and talk to me. Lorraine puts baby powder on my bottom. Ruby says I smell good. They smell good too! Perhaps they will let me use some of their lotion one day. Ruby is holding my hand. I hope they let her hold me today. We are on our way back to the sunroom. Down the hall, we see that Mom and Dad are taking the boys outside. So we follow them down the long hall through the doors. On the other side of the doors is the longest open porch. There are moms, dads, kids, and babies all visiting out here. I think they are enjoying that big yellow ball that Bobby calls the sun. He says that if I stay out here with it, I will soon look like him. I wonder why it doesn't work on Dad. The sun hurts my eyes; therefore, I'm not looking at it anymore. There is something outside that wasn't inside. I can't see it, but it keeps me cool even though the sun is hot. It makes my hair move and makes me catch my breath. Dad says there's always a good breeze on this porch. Breezes are good things!

Just over the porch railing, two butterflies are chasing each other. They look like they're having fun. There is a beautiful bird. He's standing still in midair just above a group of flowers. I like the bird. Robert and Albert are showing me a bird's nest up on the top of the porch. There are three little birds in the nest. They must be hungry. They are crying. It's no wonder Mom is excited. Sunday is my favorite day too. While everyone is watching the birds, Albert puts a wildflower on my blanket; then he runs back to play. Brothers are cute!

I see Ann. She's at the far end of the hall. She has a cart with cups, bottles, and other things on it. She must have something really good. Even the moms and dads want some. The boys want to go down to where she is, but Dad tells them to stay here until she comes to them. Now, she says, "Would the Tates like ice tea, lemonade, water, or cake and ice cream?" Of course, they want cake and ice cream. Dad gets ice tea and a small glass of water. He takes me from Lorraine so she can eat with the kids. He lays me down in his arms. He takes his white crisp handkerchief from atop his straw hat. He dips it into the water.

He brings the handkerchief in front of my mouth as he says, "Open up." When I don't respond, he places his finger on my lips. When I try to suck his finger, he squeezes a drop of water into my mouth. The cool, wet, clean taste is refreshing. It is different, and it feels smooth. It satisfies me, and I want more. I open my mouth for more. This time, he gives me two drops. They wet the inside of my mouth that is in need of their treat. Dad says, "I'm glad you like this stuff called water. It goes in here and comes out as a wet diaper. While it's between your lips and your hips, it makes you grow." He gives me a few more drops. Then he places me up against his shoulder. He walks off the porch and down onto that green blanket of grass. He follows the grass to the corner of the building. There is a stone walk that goes down a hill to something new and different. It is alive and busy. Dad says, "This is the river. It has millions of gallons of water in it." The water runs into itself with such force that I can hear it. Dad is standing under a shade of a large old tree, which shades the path to the river. I like the trees! Dad is taking me to find Mom. He says, "It's dinnertime for you." I know what's going to happen when I eat. I'm going to fall asleep and miss everything.

As we round the corner, Lorraine is playing pitch and catch with the boys. Ruby is sitting on Mom's lap as she tells her all the news. I'm resting my head on Daddy's shoulder; my face is touching his neck. He's wearing the nicest cologne. It smells better than my stuff, and everyone says, "Babies smell good." I think I want to stay right here. We are back in Mom's room where she has been waiting to feed me while the kids are outside playing. Quiet as it is kept, I'm ready to eat. The way I see it, only Christmas and Mom's and Dad's birthdays are more important than my birthday. I really like Saturdays, though I've only had one. But Sundays are the best. Sundays are special food, dress-up clothes, church, visiting family, hugs, kisses, flowers, water, hummingbirds, and butterflies. Sundays make me smile and feel loved and wanted. Right now, the sandman is coming to take me to sleep. As babies, we eat, sleep, and have our diapers changed. I hope it's still Sunday when I wake up.

It's 5:15 p.m.; we are sitting on the front porch. Dad says that it's time he gets the kids home because they have to eat dinner and get ready for school.

Robert says, "Wednesday is the last day of school." For the first time, Albert seems happy.

"No more school," he says, putting his hands together in front of his face the way Mommy does when she is thanking "the big guy," as Daddy calls him.

Mom says, "Thank God." I know Mom loves this God guy because he introduced her to Dad when they were seventeen. Mom and Dad are from North Carolina. Dad was born and raised in Gastonia, North Carolina, to James and Liza Tate, who were farmers. Dad has eleven brothers and sisters. His grandparent, Grandpa Jim, was a Caucasian man; and his wife, Grandma Sue, was full-blood Indian. This is where my dad Olen, the farmer's son, gets his features, including his freckles. Mom and Dad married in 1926.

I overheard that story this morning as Mom was talking to her friend Ann. Did I tell you? Mom works here when she's not at home waiting for me to be born. I guess she just loves babies. Mom calls the kids to say goodbye. Ruby looks like she's going to cry because she wants to stay with Mom. Mom tells her that if she smiles, she will let her hold the baby. Oh, that's me. She's not much bigger than I am. Maybe we should wait till she's sixteen. Well, I guess that smile means we are going to get together. She's sitting in the chair. Mom tells her to put one arm under my head and the other under my bottom. She's good for a little kid, and having me here makes her smile. She's so small that I can touch her face. It's soft and warm. She has two long braids with pretty bows. I reach for her bow; and she says, "Cynthia, don't pull on my bow; that's not nice." The boys are here to say goodbye. It's no wonder Dad wants to take them home. They have grass stains on their once-white shirts and dirt on their pressed pants. Their shoes are dirty too.

Dad says, "You can take them out of the country, but you can't take the country out of them." They both give me a kiss on the cheek and run to the car. Lorraine gives Mom a hug and a kiss; then, she takes me from Ruby. Mom tells Ruby she is a big girl. She's off the porch and skipping down the sidewalk toward the car. I must remember to have Ruby teach me to skip because it looks like fun.

Mom tells Dad we are coming home this week. She reminds him as though he will forget to pick us up. Lorraine gives me a kiss. Then, she hands me to Mom. Lorraine and Dad are walking toward the car. Dad's black shiny car is slipping out of sight down the driveway.

In the Heat of the Night

It's 6:05 p.m. We are all out on the porch. Ann is feeding one of the babies. The other four are being fed by their moms. Mom is telling Ann that my sisters and brothers look as though they have grown since last Thursday. Mom stops talking and Ann stops feeding the baby when the bell starts ringing. Ann says that means there's a fire. One of the guys who works in the kitchen just runs out on the porch. He yells to the nurses that this is a real fire and that they should get all the patients out of the hospital immediately. The bell is louder now, and it almost sounds like one continuous noise. All I know is that we don't like it; all the babies are crying. People are coming from everywhere! They are helping the nurses get the patients out. One of the nurses collects our medications, records, and diapers while assisting patients during the evacuation. Mom says the fire truck had better get here soon or this old wood frame house will burn down. The two ambulances are taking the four patients who are seriously ill away from the hospital. All the patients have been helped out. They are down by the front gate. Mom, the other mothers, and babies are the first ones down there. One of the guys from the kitchen just tells Mom that the whole back of the hospital is engulfed in flames now and still no fire trucks have arrived. Finally, two trucks with their horns screaming are coming up in the driveway.

The flames are coming out the windows as well as from the back of the hospital. The trucks are going across the front lawn, down the south side of the garage to reach the river.

It seems like forever since peace and quiet were interrupted by the fire bell, and not one drop of water has reached the flames. The back porch, kitchen, and dining area just crash to the ground. The flames are coming through the roof in the middle of the house. Finally, water is streaming from the hoses. The water seems to be making matters worse, as smoke is billowing out of every opening. Ann says, "It's time for us to leave." The flames are climbing so high in the sky that we can feel the heat down here. I'm glad we are leaving because I don't like the smoke. Ed, the groundskeeper, has a big station wagon; and he's going to drive us to another hospital. Mom and I are getting into the front seat. She has me up on her shoulder from this position I can still see the fire. The large front hospital doors are open. The fire has burned through the walls. I see beds, tables, and chairs standing in rooms that now have no walls. The firemen are pulling their hoses back and yelling that the roof is collapsing. The collapse of the roof creates a plume of smoke and debris that form a large black cloud. The smell of smoke is so thick in the air that it makes breathing labored. We are being taken to a small home for seniors. The doctors say all the babies and moms can go home except us. Mom and I have to stay here until tomorrow to have her stitches removed. It's almost dark outside. The nurses have called the families of my five little friends. Only one baby and his mom are left. Mom says, "We smell like smoke," so she is going to bathe us. Because there's a shortage of beds, I'm going to sleep with her.

It must be 7:00 a.m. The night nurses are leaving as the day nurses are coming in. Mom and I have been up long enough to bathe and have breakfast. Mom has been waiting till 7:00 p.m. to call Dad. Dad is a brick baker who works from 4:00 a.m. till noon. Mom says she will catch him on his lunch break. Dad says that he heard the fire trucks and saw the smoke, but he thinks some farmer's barn was burning. Mom asks Dad to bring us clean clothes to wear home since we lost everything in the fire. At 9:00 a.m., the funny little doctor comes to remove Mom's stitches and give us a final checkup. He tells Mom we were clear for takeoff. He tells her to make an appointment to see him in six weeks. Just as quickly as he appears, he disappears down the hall.

Mom is sitting in a rocking chair on the small front porch. From inside the open window, I hear a radio. The announcer is saying it's Monday, June 16; it's eighty-one degrees at 1:25 p.m. here in sunny Saugerties. People here still can't believe Dales Hospital is no more. Mom says I was the last baby delivered there! Due to the fire, Mom and the nurses no longer have jobs. Ann says the owners are looking for a new location. By the time Mom is ready to go back to work, they will have a new hospital.

Dad just pulled up in the parking lot. He has one bag in each hand and a small yellow teddy bear under his arm. He looks happy to see us, and I am glad we are leaving.

Dad says, "Good afternoon, ladies."

Mom says, "You are a sight for sore eyes." (She means her eyes are tired from looking for him.) Ann smiles, and they exchange hellos. Ann takes the bags from Dad, Mom opens the door, and we go inside to change clothes. Looking over Mom's shoulder, I see Dad. He's sitting in the rocking chair, and he's still holding that little yellow teddy bear. Now that we are dressed in clothes that smell April fresh, Mom brings me outside and places me in his lap. Then, she says that she is going back inside to schedule an appointment and to say goodbye to the nurses.

As soon as she disappears behind the screen door, Dad says, "This is for you, baby girl." He places in my arms the small bear he has been holding. He strokes the small teddy bear and says, "See, it won't hurt you. Now, you have something to hold when I'm not holding you." A few minutes later, Mom returns, and we are ready to go home.

At last, I'm going to get a ride in Dad's new black Oldsmobile. It's even nicer inside than outside because it has soft leather seats, it smells new, and its ride is silky smooth. He tells Mom that the workmen are already busy tearing down what's left of the hospital. He stops the car at the entrance to where Dales Hospital once stood. All that remains is a brick chimney, charred tin from the roof, and a pile of black smoldering wood. Other cars slow down or stop to look in disbelief at the place where generations of people were born.

Homeward Bound

The windows are down in the car. The breeze feels good on my face. Outside, there are trees, flowers, and crystal-clear blue skies. A large brown horse is eating grass in the field. We only live three or four miles from the hospital. I imagined it to be much farther. Dad says that he has to stop at the store to buy bread and milk. We then go to the post office to pick up the mail. While on Main Street, I see the grade school, a small movie theater, and an old church. Dad turns left off Main Street and down a lane that has a football field on one side and a softball field on the other. Beyond the fields of lush green grass are five or six houses. Our house is a gray two-story wood structure at the end of the lane. He parks the car in front of the garage; then, he comes around to open the door so Mom can get out. Outside the car, a cute little bird dog, with tail wagging, waits for his turn to welcome Mom home. Champ is dad's hunting dog. He's cute! Just that quick, people are congregating outside our house. Our next-door neighbors and three of their twelve kids are here to meet me and to welcome Mom home. Their eldest daughter and her husband are expecting their first baby and are amazed at how small I am. Within minutes, there are eight people checking me out. Babies must be important little people because everyone wants to see and touch them.

So this is home! It's all green grass and trees, blue skies, and people with great tans. There are birds, butterflies, and crickets. Mom is taking me inside now. Downstairs on the right is the living room and bedrooms. She's going upstairs now. There is a large eat-in kitchen and yet another bedroom. Out the kitchen window, apple trees, peach trees, and cherry trees dot the landscape. Large weeping willow trees grow in groups that resemble families. Smaller groups of pine trees of various shapes and sizes stand still in the afternoon sun. The unkept long grass fills the space between the trees. Wildflowers and flowering weeds add a dash of color to the many shades of green. Beyond this half mile of greenery, the landscape slopes gradually, then levels off before it meets the riverbanks. The river is wider and calmer here at home. It is the same river that flowed behind Dales Hospital. Mom takes me into their room. Outside the window, I see so many beautiful things. Just across the lane at the end of our driveway is a nature garden. Soft wildflowers sway in the gentle breeze. Beautiful flowers of pale yellow, violet, and sky blue share their space with bright yellow sunflowers and Brown-Eyed-Susans. Just beyond the flowers is a cornfield that covers the mile or so between home and the mountains. Each row of corn stands at attention in perfect formation. Each stalk resembles soldiers wearing their dress green uniforms. The bright yellow corns are their medals of honor. The large upper leaves wave gently like arms in formation. The most breathtaking beautiful mountains rise up as though reaching to touch the summer sky. Already, home is by far the best of all places. Dad is going to pick the kids up from school. Champ is asleep at the head of the stairs, and Mom is making coffee. The combination of the summer breeze and the aroma of the brewing coffee are making me sleepy. For the first time, I'm going to sleep knowing love is my lifetime connection to my new family. When I wake up, we will all be together at home for the first time.

It's three thirty in the afternoon, and our once-quiet house is quiet no more. Dad is back with the kids, and they know we came home today. Champ hears them running up the stairs as he takes cover under the kitchen table. Each of the children runs to Mom for a hug to make sure she really is home. When they are satisfied, she tells them that dinner is at four thirty. She tells them to change their clothes before dinner. Food must be great stuff; just that quick, they are gone. Lorraine is the first to return. She notices me lying in the middle of the bed; then, she comes in to join me. Now, all four of my sisters and brothers are on the bed with me. Mom just told Dad that they are having smothered steak with mashed potatoes and gravy, hot biscuits, corn, and tomatoes.

THE FIRST FAMILY MEAL

Whatever this stuff called food is, it sure smells good. As Mom would say, even the aroma tastes good.

Robert is sitting on the foot of the bed. He says, "I'm glad Mom is home. Smothered steak is my favorite food and sweet tea my favorite drink." I can't wait to see what sweet tea looks like. Today, the kids got their final report cards. They all pass to the next grade. Dad says Albert is going to need extra help with his math during the summer. Lorraine seems to have the most trouble with school. She'd like to quit school and get a job.

Mom says, "We will discuss school after dinner. Dinner is in ten minutes!" Lorraine is the first to change, wash her hands, and return. She comes in the bedroom, picks me up, and carries me into the kitchen.

There is a large table with a tablecloth, dishes, silverware, glasses, and napkins. I like the many colors, like red sliced tomato, green lettuce, yellow corn, golden brown rolls with bright yellow butter easing over their sides, steak smothered in brown gravy, and string beans with potatoes. In the middle of the table are two pitchers of sweet tea with lemon and ice.

Robert comes into the kitchen, spots the ice tea, and with a smile, he announces, "That's mine." Mom tells them to sit down and eat before the food gets cold. She takes me from Lorraine and sits down in a chair next to the open window. Looking down, I can see Dad has a garden with string beans, tomatoes, corn, and potatoes. He also has a few chickens in a coop behind the garage. The boys' bicycles and roller skates are all in a row next to the side of the garage. The grass in the backyard looks as though it were freshly mowed today. I hope they take me out there! Green is one of my favorite colors. Everyone has food on his plate, and Dad has blessed the food. I like the blessing! That's the first time I've heard a blessing. Someone has to teach me to do that when I learn to talk. Robert is going for one of the pitchers of ice tea. Mom gives him a smile and a wink. Food must be good stuff because the kids aren't talking anymore. They eat what they want from their plates and leave the rest.

When Mom is satisfied that they have had enough to eat, she says, "When the kitchen is clean, I have a surprise for you."

FAMILY

All the kids help clean the table. Dad helps them put the food away. As the boys take the trash out, Lorraine washes the dishes, while Robert dries them, and Albert waits to sweep the floor. Ruby stands on a step stool, putting the silverware in the drawer. While they finish cleaning the kitchen, Mom takes me into her room to change and feed me. I was wrong about Sunday. Monday at home is the greatest. Today, I learned that a home is a world all its own. It's unlike any other place you will ever know. Good, bad, or indifferent, it is yours. I'm almost two weeks old; and already, I've had a ride in a car, met our neighbors, met our dog, got my first smell of real food, and I know where my family lives. I arrive home in time to hear Dad bless the meal, and if it tastes half as good as the aroma, "God bless the cook" is my prayer. Tonight, I'm going to enjoy my special food; but I'm going to start praying for teeth, if you know what I mean. All I know is that I'm not ever leaving home! Mom and I come into the kitchen as she thanks Dad and the kids for cleaning up for her. On her way to the icebox, mom stops long enough to place me on my father's lap then she goes to the icebox, takes out a large container, and places it on the table. She takes a stack of small plates to put a scoop of ice cream onto each one. Next, she adds cookies to each plate. She makes a plate for each of the kids and one for Dad. Once again, those four chatterboxes are quiet. She tells the kids they can go out to play when they finished eating.

Mom announces, "It's time for Cynthia and me to take a nap." She takes me into her room, lays me on her bed, pulls the shades down to block out the sun, and then joins me on the bed. As I lay there, I think I've seen and learned so many things from the people I've met, and I know there is so much more. I wonder how long before I get teeth, when I will grow hair, and when will I be able to talk to them. When will

I be able to walk, run, skip, and drink sweet tea? I hope it's soon. Well, it's been one of those days that Mom has shared a part of her with me. She has changed my diaper, and she has given me one of her special mommy kisses; so you know what time it is the sandman is coming. Daddy says I grow when I sleep. I hope so because that's exactly what I'm going to do.

A Message to Mommy

At last, I'm home, and everything is wonderful here. Well, almost everything! Mom, now that we are home alone, I need to communicate with you. Back when I was in my home in the womb, back when I was a work in progress, I ate "good"—much better than I do now. I didn't say anything before because I thought all they knew how to fix at the hospital was milk and water. When they tried to cook, they burned the place down to the ground. I recall when I was in the womb that we had eggs, bacon, fish, potato salad, Mac and cheese, chicken, steak, and great sweet treats. Now that I'm a real live little grown-up, all I get is milk, milk, milk. I've had so much of that stuff that I can't keep it down. I know I don't have teeth, but if I can eat that stuff in those little jars with that picture of that little baby with the big smile, I can eat food cooked today. Do you know how old that stuff is in those jars? That kid on the bottle is thirty-six years old. The carrots taste like wet straw, and the green peas have vanished with only their skin remaining.

Mom, I know you don't think anyone is at home in here simply because I can't talk, but I'm in here. Mom, we have issues! Do you ever wonder why I push my bottle away? I'm trying to tell you that it's enough already! Back when I was in the womb, I don't ever remember one glass of moo juice coming down the pike, and look at me—I'm healthy. Mom, I've had enough of that baby stuff. I don't want to be rude, spitting up on nice people because that stuff won't stay down. Four bottles of milk before noon would make the cow who gave it sick.

Let's make a deal. Let's start the morning off with juice. I don't need teeth to drink juice. Don't try to trick me because I saw Grandma drink juice, and her teeth are in a jar in the bathroom.

Okay! If I just have to have milk, right next to the white milk is a bottle called chocolate milk. Now that's good stuff. It's so good that they make ice cream out of it. Have you ever seen a frozen white milk bar? It probably won't freeze. Just for a change, let the kids drink my milk and give me their chocolate milk.

Mom, I'm flexible; if that won't work, let's put some cornflakes in a bowl. Pour some *milk* over them, add some sugar, and wait for those flakes to soften up. Take that little spoon that you give me medicine with and shovel . . . um . . . on home. I can eat those things; really, I can. Come on, try me. After all that conversation, guess what I had for breakfast? You guessed it: bad milk and that tired stuff in those little jars. I just can't figure out what that baby is smiling about. Mom, I notice that when you are cooking, you taste the food. How come you never taste that stuff in those little jars? Could it be that you know how bad it really is? And another thing. These kids would eat air if they could catch it between two slices of bread. If my stuff is so good, how come they don't touch it? If you didn't make me drink all that milk, I wouldn't get sick, need my back rubbed, or throw up on my clean clothes. In case you haven't noticed, it stinks too.

Well, it's almost lunchtime, so I am going to try again. "Baby to Mommy!" It's your brown-eyed little beauty calling. Come on, Mom, give a girl a break. Dump the dairy and fill this little bottle with sweet tea. Could you see your way clear to break me off a piece of that baked haddock and throw in a spoon of those creamy mashed potatoes? Okay, give me the spinach too. See, I'm a good sport. Mom, if you would listen to me, we could speed up this growth schedule. This milk and water fasting is starving me. I hope this conversation bears more fruit than our breakfast chat.

We must have gotten disconnected. Here she comes with those little jars, with little miss-smiley face on them; and of course, we can't forget the cow's contribution.

Parents are supposed to be smart. Why don't they get it? When I throw my bottle on the floor, that means I don't want it. Dad picks it up, washes it, and gives it back to me so many times that I'm tired for him. If I throw it again, he will only pick it up again.

I hear Mom's friend say that she was up all night with William. If she gives him eight bottles of milk a day, take my word, his stomach is making more noise than a marching band.

Have you ever watched your mom check the expiration date on the milk carton? Then, just to make you feel better, give it the old sniff test. She stops just short of drinking it. So what does she do? Without so much as shaking it up, she pours that configuration into a bottle and gives it to you. Here I am, all of twenty-one days old, and I'm already testing milk. Well, I'm tired of trying to get through these two. I'm going to take a nap while my stomach is calm. Mommies, if you have a newborn, *please* put some variety into the menu! How would you like to eat the same thing for three weeks? Remember, we don't have jobs; we don't go to school; we don't run, walk; and we can't even crawl. But we can see, smell, hear, taste, and feel.

Let me tell you a little story. Last New Year's Eve, I was in my twelfth week in the womb. Mom and Dad took me to a New Year's Eve party. At midnight, Mom had a small cup of beer. Now, that was exciting. I don't know if it was the brew or the bubbles, but I was mellow and calm for three days. Personally, I think a little brew in the bottle would definitely help take the edge off. It's not like we are going to crawl into something, fall, or drive while under the influence.

Well, dinner has come and gone, and gone is the best part of that line. The only way milk is eliminated from my menu is if cows go on strike and refuse to give it up.

Let me clue ya. Things are different for babies. We see the world differently. We do everything lying down. We get a bath lying down. Have you tried that lately? What would your spouse think if he comes into the bedroom and finds you lying on the bed putting your underwear on or rolling from side to side putting your shirt on? When was the last time someone tried to shove a washcloth in your ear?

Hey, listen, my eight-year-old brother is afraid of the dark, but because he can talk, they leave the light on in his room. I'm twenty-one days old. They not only turn the light off, but they also close the door. I wonder what they think I'm going to do to keep them up talking loud or singing all night. The first night I woke up in that dark room, I think to myself that I am back in the womb.

Then, there is that big yellow ball outside the window. It looks like it has a face. It doesn't move, so we just stare at each other. Then, it goes behind a cloud. I think I have won! My heart jumps back into my chest, and I start to breathe again. Just about the time I feel normal, it is back again. This time, he is closer and bigger. This time, it wins! I scream until someone comes to get me out of there. Then, there are the night shadows, like things in the room, a hat on the back of the door, or a balloon on a string moving in the dark.

The darkness is a scary place. How would you like to wake up to find someone checking your diaper in the dark? You don't know what to do. Shall I hold my breath or scream?

Imagine these, I am twenty-one days old and twenty-seven inches long. The kids have me on the floor. We have a dog. Everyone walks upright on two legs. The dog walks on four legs. Now, he stands over me a few inches away from my face, and his beady eyes are right in front of me. They say that I don't like the dog when, in reality, I don't know the dog or what it plans to do next. It's not fair. I'm the only one here with no teeth, can't speak, or can't walk. After watching him for weeks, the fear fades away. Now, I look for him every morning. I *really* begin to like him when he starts sleeping in that dark room with me. Today, they take me for a ride in the car. Why do they do this? They strap me into a car seat, lying down, of course. All I can see are the tops of houses, the tops of trees, and streetlights. No one talks to me, so I go to sleep.

Why is it that people dismiss babies? They introduce everyone to everyone else; then, they say and that's Beatrix.

You're lying there, saying, "I didn't catch your name, big guy. Could you run that by me again?" They ignore you and go on talking to each other.

Grown-ups have no idea what we are thinking. I think it's time they knew!

1. Food—let us try it. If we spit it at you, that means you save your time and money. We don't want it anymore!
2. Since you and the doctors aren't drinking eight glasses of milk every day, please give us something else like juice or tea, please!
3. Please don't let those crazy kids handle knives.
4. Please don't let them warm the bottle because they take *warm* to a whole new level. They make milk like hot lava, and it burns my new pipes.
5. Mommies, please ask your friends who haven't shaved to keep their stickers off my delicate skin.
6. Please, don't pull me up by my arms! These joints are new and fragile. It feels like they are ripping them out of their sockets. I really don't want to scream on them.
7. By the way, could you turn me on my side every three or four hours? My back and buns are killing me.
8. Could ya ask your friends not to put so much toilet water on? It's sickening! They might want to put more of it in the toilet.
9. Do you ever wonder why babies sleep better and longer during the day? First, at night it's dark, and we are afraid of the dark. Then, you put us in a room and close the door. There really is a boogeyman, ya know!
10. Please remember to *turn the light* on when you come into my room *or* get a clapper.
11. About that phone, why does everyone have to yell *telephone* as loud as they can? Don't they know what a phone is?

12. Can you turn the phone off after nine because I'm trying to sleep.

13. Mom, please don't put the phone to my ear again. First, I don't know those crazy people on the other end who are trying to talk like a baby. They keep asking me questions as though they're expecting me to answer them.

14. How come the air conditioner is in your room? What's up with that? Babies don't like it hot either.

15. When you take me out in my carriage, I notice you have sunglasses on. I'm lying down. The sun is shining in my eyes all the time. It's so bright that I can see it through my eyelids.

16. Could you flip that top over so it can block the sun? And I'd like some sunglasses too.

17. When I'm looking up at the ceiling, it's because the sun has blinded me.

18. Could somebody give the dog a bath since you can't take that fur coat off?

19. Please, I want no more tickling the feet or pinching the cheeks. That's not funny. Oh, it's time for table food, okay!

20. Please, leave the TV on the cartoon channel.

THE FOURTH OF JULY

Days turn into weeks. Already, it's July 4. Lorraine is telling Ruby there is going to be a cookout today with fireworks tonight. People stop by to eat, drink, play games, and talk. Today, I meet Mom's brother Jay Van and his wife, Margaret. Ruby says that he is our uncle and that she is our aunt. Uncle Van is a tall dark-skinned man. He is pencil thin and smokes a pipe. He is a quiet, soft-spoken man who looks a lot like Mom. Aunt Margaret is a short round light-skinned woman who never stops talking. While alone in the kitchen, Aunt Margaret, who has no children of her own, voices her opinion regarding whether Mom needs more children. Suppose Mom had listened to her, I would not be at this party. So far, I'm not feeling her at all, but I'm going to give her a chance. Mom tells her she doesn't need her permission to have a baby. I think that should hold her for a while. Robert is telling Dad the fireworks are almost ready to start. He seems excited about fireworks. In a flash, he runs downstairs and outside again. Dad yells after him, "Make sure Champ is in the house. You know he hates that noise."

Robert yells back, "Okay, Dad, I will bring him in now so he doesn't run away." Robert laughs as he carries Champ into the house. He says, "You have to stay in because you ran away last year." Robert is back outside with two of the boys from next door. It's dusk. All the neighbors, their friends, and people from all around are outside waiting for this noise called fireworks. After a few minutes, a red light leaves the ground and shoots upward toward the sky. Seconds later, a yellow one follows and goes up a little higher. This one has a boom at the end of its flight. Now, three of those rockets go up higher. They open up and have a louder boom. Each rocket goes higher and higher, and the boom gets louder and louder. Now, many rockets go up one after another, and the boom is as loud as thunder. Next, I see why Champ wants to run away. All the dogs in the neighborhood are howling. The ones that are outside are running away from the noise. I like the pretty colors of the fireworks, but I don't like the noise. It frightens me too. Mom is taking me inside.

She says that the noise is too loud for me. She closes the windows, and she holds me up against her breasts. Looking in the mirror on her dresser, I still see the lights from the fireworks. Poor Champ, he is hiding under the boys' bed, howling because the noise frightens him. If I could, I would open the door so he could run away from the noise. Finally, the lights and noise stop just as quickly as it had started. It's over. Families, lovers, and kids walk back to their cars or homes. The kids are now home. They are running up the stairs. Mom tells them to take their baths and get ready for bed. Bobby and Albert are talking about the last group of fireworks. They go higher and make more noise than all the rest.

The kids are bathed and in their rooms. Mom is lying down resting, and Dad is sitting in his rocking chair, listening to the ball game. Peace and quiet have returned to Gray Fox Lane. Through the open window, I see my friend, the man in the moon. He is surrounded by thousands of shimmering summer stars. They glow like diamonds. They form the Big Dipper, a little one, and a highway to heaven. The crickets and bullfrogs are back, and they are providing music to sleep by. I have had more than enough excitement this day. So I think I will go to sleep too. I'm sure they have much to show and teach me tomorrow, and I could stand to grow a few inches.

THE FIRST CHRISTMAS

August is followed by September. School starts for the kids, and the seasons change. The beautiful leaves that once were a blanket for the trees change colors, fall, and now look like an endless watercolor painting spread out to dry on a mat of green grass. Someday, I hope I will be able paint in colors like those I see from the window of Mommy and Daddy's room. The sun and the mountains in the distance make this the most beautiful picture I've ever seen.

Halloween and Thanksgiving come and go. It's Christmas Eve. Mom is explaining the meaning of Christmas to Ruby. She wants to know why she is getting presents from Santa Claus when it's Christ's birthday. Dad says that I've been asking her that question for years! This morning, Dad takes the boys out into the woods. They pick a Christmas tree, and then, they cut it down and carry it home. Lorraine has been decorating it all day. She calls from downstairs. She wants us to come down to see the tree. Mom picks me up off the bed, while Dad takes Ruby, and they carry us downstairs. When we come around the corner, the beauty of the tree almost takes my breath away.

Lorraine observes the look on my face and says, "The baby likes the tree; she's smiling." The colored balls and the shimmering icicles fascinate me. Maybe people give Christ pretty trees for his birthday. I like Christmas trees; and when I grow a little more, I want to help Lorraine decorate one. All day long, they say Santa Claus is coming tonight. I guess they forgot to tell him that I go to bed early. Dad tells the kids if they want Santa to come, they had better go to bed. As he is explaining why they should go to sleep, I'm falling asleep right here in my mother's arms. Mom and Dad are almost upstairs now, and I'm more asleep than awake. I hope this Santa Claus guy that the kids are waiting for doesn't awaken me! I need my rest, if I'm ever going to grow.

It seems that I just fell asleep because it's still dark outside. It's warm here in my bed. Dad says it's 6:30 a.m. The kids are up, and they can't wait another minute to see what Santa left them. Dad says, "This Santa guy works one day a year, yet he doesn't have normal hours." Dad wants to go back to sleep, but the boys aren't going to leave him alone. Before his feet hit the floor, they are halfway down the stairs. There are presents that talk, walk, and play music. There are trucks with horns; there are books, clothes, and funny slippers.

All I have to say is that it looks like a cyclone hit our living room. There are boxes, wrapping paper, and bows everywhere. Next year, I think I'm going to stay up to meet this guy called Santa Claus. He gives out really nice presents. The kids don't seem to notice the mess that they are making. They are testing every present as if it were a play period at school. I haven't seen them this happy over anything since I've been home. I guess kids getting presents and enjoying them must be Christ's present to them on his birthday. Mom and Dad have a happy, content little smile on their faces as though this is good! They are going back upstairs. I don't think they can take the noise or the mess the kids made in the living room. Dad puts the shade up in the kitchen and sees snow. He tells Mom that it really is Christmas. We got ten inches or more of snow during the night. He says it's starting to snow again. Mom carries me over to the window. The snowflakes are big, pure white, and fluffy. They float past the window on their way down to the ground below. I like the snow. I could watch it fall all day.

Mom says, "There is nothing quite like a blanket of new snow on Christmas Eve." She says that it looks like a Christmas card.

There is a huge bowl of fruit on the table. There are pretty colors and different size fruit in it. Dad is peeling an orange.

Mom hands me to him and says, "It looks as though we are up; so, I guess I had better feed the kids. It must take a lot of energy to make a mess like the one they have down there." Soon, there is the smell of bacon and coffee in the air. Golden brown pancakes are stacked on a plate. Bright yellow butter melts from the heat of the pancakes and slides over them. Milk and juice fill the once empty glasses on the table. Mom scrambles eggs, and a breakfast fit for a king is about to meet the family. Dad calls the kids. They are too excited with the toys and want to continue playing. Dad announces that this is the one and only breakfast being served here today. With that they come to the table. This Christmas is perfect in every way.

For some time now, I have been sitting on my father's lap at mealtime. Today is no exception. This morning, I watch them eat, but for the first time, I extend my hand to Dad's plate. I take a small piece of his eggs and put it in my mouth. It is different from baby food or milk. I decide that I like the taste. Next, I try the pancakes; maybe it is the sweet taste of the syrup. Today pancakes become a breakfast favorite for me. From that day on, I eat off my dad's plate until they give me one of my own. After breakfast, the kids take me downstairs. I get to see them play with their toys and mine. Of all the toys, I like the radio and the record player. I wonder where the people are who are singing or talking. It is magic that the kids can turn them on and off whenever they want. To me it is magic!

Lorraine carries me over to the window. She opens it to let me touch the snow. I am surprised that it is cold and wet; yet, I still like to look at it. That afternoon, the kids get dressed to go outside to play in the snow. They throw snowballs at each other; and they make snowmen. Next, they sleigh ride for hours. I decide snow is fun stuff for kids, and I would like to play in it with them. After what seems like forever, they come back inside. They are cold and wet, but they are happy. Mom makes them hot chocolate and instructs them to put on dry clothes. After the Christmas feast, the kids calm down and read stories from the books that they received from Santa Claus. This has been the most exciting day of my life, and I'm looking forward to the next one.

Mom's Greatest Gifts (Music)

It's 9:00 a.m. Palm Sunday morning. As usual, in our house breakfast is over, and the dishes are done. Like every Sunday, everyone is busy getting ready for the eleven o'clock church services. As always, Mom has dressed me first. So, I'm watching her put her makeup on. She decides which jewelry she wants to wear and puts it on. She combs her hair one more time. Then, she put a drop of perfume behind each ear and one on each wrist. She reaches in her purse, comes out with a gold tube of lipstick, lines her lips, and then blots them. That's amazing! How did she do that? Satisfied, she picks up her hat, gloves, and bag. She looks in the full length mirror to make sure everything is just right. Standing before that mirror wearing a warm yellow silk suit, bone colored silk blouse, and matching shoes, Momma is beautiful. She's wearing her favorite pearls around her neck with matching pearl earrings. I love to watch her walk. That switch in her walk and that pop in her skirt give the hem something to do other than just hold the bottom of her skirt. Finally, she is satisfied with her appearance; now we are ready for church.

This morning, we aren't going to our church. Mom and Dad have been Methodist all of their lives. Methodists are quiet, reserved, cool people. The choir, though sixty strong, sings as though they are in a library. The Reverend Dawson is a sixty-one-year-old man with a cotton-soft voice and a mild manner. This church is a baby's dream. Since I can't hear what he is saying, this is the perfect place for a morning nap. I must be special, because Mom lets me sleep in church. Every time one of the other kids closes both eyes at one time, she wakes them up to that look that means "not here and not now." This library-soft music is perfect for sleeping.

This morning, we are going to church with Uncle Van and Aunt Margaret. They are born and bred Baptist up from the south. This is going to be my first visit to a Baptist church. Dad drives us the nine miles from our house to the church. When we arrive, Sunday school has just ended. There are kids of all ages and sizes playing on the manicured lawn next to the church. Older kids supervise the younger kids at play. Just that quickly, Robert and Albert join a group of boys playing catch. Thick deep green hedges separate the kids from the sidewalk and the street. Pretty colored flowers adorn the entire grounds on all sides of the building. Beautiful tall stained-glass windows of blue, red, green, and yellow filter light in from both sides. The top front of the church is a steeple that holds a gold cross. I wonder how and who put it up there? The front of the church has steps that are as wide as the building. They are rounded on each end with a wrought iron rail down the middle. There are two sets of huge heavy oak doors with rounded tops, six panel glass panes, and large gold knobs. Two concrete pots filled with soft yellow flowers combine to make a grand exterior to this church. This church has character, beauty, life, and energy. The people are genuinely happy to see each other. Unlike the Methodist church, kids laugh, talk, and play here. I decide here and now that when I am old enough, I want to be a Baptist. People stand laughing, talking, and embracing in front of this large stone structure. Aunt Margaret and Uncle Van come out of the crowd and over to where Mom and Dad are visiting with people they know from North Carolina.

Mom asks Ruby to go get the boys, saying, "It's time for church to start." By the way, Ruby is five years old. Unlike the other kids, she doesn't play when she has her Sunday clothes on because she hates to get dirty or mess up her clothes. She gets that from Mom. Ruby is going to be a model when she grows up. I hope it's okay for models to be shy, because she's too shy that she doesn't talk to herself.

Slowly, with head lowered, she walks over to Robert and announces, "Mom would like you and Albert to come on." To insure she does as she is told, she takes his hand and walks him back to Mom. All the kids are back with their families, who are busy making last-minute adjustments to them. Promptly at eleven o'clock, both sets of oak doors open as though by magic. Mom hands me to Dad so that he can carry me up the stairs. Mom is holding Ruby's hand. Lorraine and the boys are walking ahead of us with Uncle Van. Dad has me standing up in his arms. From this position, I can see everything. Once we pass through those doors, I see the four ushers who opened them, standing in front of the now-open doors. The church vestibule is a large friendly area with coat racks, two benches, one on each side, and two open stained glass windows. A visitor's book and pen are on a tall table by the door.

When I turn to look in front of us, I see the world's largest pipe organ. Its pipes go all the way up to the ceiling. It is awesome! I think to myself as Dad walks into the body of the church; so, that's where that sweet sound that signals the beginning of the service comes from. My next thought is, it must take a couple of big guys to make music come out of these pipes. When we reach our seats, there before us, standing in the isle facing us, is Aunt Margaret. She is wearing all white, including white gloves, and she's carrying a fan in one hand. She smiles as Uncle Van approaches her. Using the fan, she gestures her desire that we be seated in this isle. Uncle Van, being Mom's brother, has the same joking playful manner.

He says, "So, what if we don't want to sit here Margaret?" As she waves him into the isle, she mumbles almost in a whisper, "The more I pray for that man, the crazier he gets." Once we are seated, Dad hands me back to Mom. She lets me sit with my back against her breast. She put her arms around me; then, she straightens my bows.

She whispers in my ear, "Did I tell you that you're the sweetest baby in the house, and you're cute too!" She always knows how to make me smile. As the rest of the families are being seated, I decide to check out this new church.

The pulpit and altar are down lower than the seats where we sit. The choir stand is on both sides of the church. Behind the pulpit stands that organ with those giant pipes. Beautiful floral arrangements dress the altar. A red velvet rope marks the three stairs that lead up to the choir stand and that organ. During this time of seating, soft music, like that played in the Methodist church, drifts over the room.

Well, it must be that time. Aunt Margaret just ushered a cute little boy of sixteen or seventeen down to the steps that lead up to the choir stand. He's wearing a blue suit, white shirt, red tie, and black shoes. Two little girls sitting in front of us are saying, "There's Uncle Pierre." Everyone calls him Master Pee! I wonder why they call him that. Maybe it's easier than Pierre! Finally, Pee Wee finishes crossing the floor. He's heading to the center of the stage, where that giant organ sits. Someone might want to tell this kid not to mess with that thing. Nobody is saying a word! Instead, they look as though someone is about to give them their favorite treat. Even the kids are leaning forward in their seats in anticipation of whatever is to come. Well, Pee Wee sits down on the stool in front of that giant organ. He flips a few switches, places his tiny hands high over the keys, nods his head, and then let his fingers down onto the keys. I shall never forget the feeling that went through every part of my being. It filled me with excitement and wonder. This is not the time for a nap; instead, I feel as though I am being carried away, floating free in the midst of the music. His fingers seem to glide first across the lower keys and then the upper ones. He hit one note three times; then he begins to play the most beautiful music I'd ever heard. It is at this point that a handsome middle-age man dressed in a long robe and carrying a Bible leads a choir of angels down the isle. The very first choir member, a tall woman with a strong, smooth, polished voice, begins singing words that were meant to accompany this heavenly sound. As the choir marches and sings, that little boy sitting in front of that organ plays music that makes one think an entire orchestra is performing. By the time he finished playing people are standing, waving, clapping, crying, and praising God. It is on this day and in this place that I first listen to my heart and feel its excitement. Today, I know Mom's friend "the big guy" has blessed the organ player. Long after the choir is seated, he continues to play his magic. It seems he can move mountains with his music. The minister stands up, steps to the podium and welcomes everyone to God's house. He then requests another selection from the choir. I really like this man; I can hear him, and he knows what to say. This time, Master Pee, as he will forever be to me, turns that organ into flutes, trumpets, violins, drums, bells, and anything he needs to make one clap, rock, or pat ones foot, sing, or otherwise feel the spirit. Mom is patting my legs with her hands to the beat of Master Pee's music. It feels good. So, I do the same to the back of her hands. Each time Master Pee strokes that giant organ something new, alive and wondrous flows from those pipes. I want him to continue playing forever. Somewhere in between the music, the minister preaches and prays. Just before the services end Master Pee and his sister Lenora sing a duet called, *Where Would I Be*. The sound of their voices, Pee's music and the message in the words seem to float boundlessly, first in my mind, then to a special place in the soul of mama's fifth seed. I hope that it always remains a part of me. This is one special Sunday! How can I tell someone that I like this church, these people, and this music? How will I get back to this place of wonder? The minister concludes the services with the blessing of the palms, followed by the benediction.

In a special announcement he says, "Today is Master Pee's eighteenth birthday. We invite you to join his biological and his church family in celebrating Master Pee's coming of age. Come meet the little man who makes big music" I hope we can stay! It is Aunt Margaret who convinces Mom and Dad to stay. I am glad I gave her a chance to redeem herself for trying to tell Mom that she didn't need anymore kids.

MEETING THE MUSIC MAKER

The kids just want to play, but I want to meet Master Pee. After dinner, everyone goes outside for Master Pee's birthday party. There are rows and rows of long tables, dressed with white table clothes with gold musical notes on them. There are balloons, streamers, gifts, and cards. In the center of a table is a beautiful cake shaped like his organ pipes and all! Large bowls of fruit salad and cool drinks sit at both ends of every table. The choir and the entire congregation sing "Happy Birthday" to Master Pee. He cuts the first piece of cake and gives it with a kiss to his mom. The many ladies in white then serve everyone. Laughing, talking, hugging, or shaking hands as he goes, Master Pee walks from table to table. After what seems like an eternity, he approaches our table. He smiles at Mom; then he kisses her gently on the cheek.

She smiles her "I'm proud of you" smile and says, "You are even better than I remember." He tries his best to look serious as he replies, "Does that mean I will see you here more often, Mrs. Tate? If I could, I would say Amen, and we will be back every Sunday. He excuses himself, shakes hands, and talks with Lorraine, then Ruby and the boys. Next, he shakes hands with Dad saying, "I'd sure like muscles like yours Mr. T." Still laughing, he turns and then comes back to Mom. I was beginning to think I was invisible, since I'm the one who wants to meet him. "So, Mrs. Tate, this is little Cynthia that my mom has been telling me about." As though he had known me forever, he picks me up from my mother's lap and says, "So, cutie, what did you like best, the music or the party?" When he says music, I give him my best baby smile.

My brother Robert, now standing next to Pee, says, "She loves music, especially piano and organ."

Pee replies, "Speaking of music, I must go turn the organ off." Master Pee asks Dad if Robert and I can accompany him. Dad says yes, and for that I thank God! Pee picks me up in his arms and carries me across the grass, and then into the side door of the church. We go down a few steps to cross the stage to the organ. That organ was huge from our seats in the middle of the church, but standing here before it, it is awesome! I could crawl up into the center pipes and have room to play. There are hundreds of black and white keys and almost as many switches on a pad. Master Pee asks Robert to hold me for one minute while he takes care of his baby.

He sits down on the stool and flips some switches on the pad. Robert, as though reading my mind, steps closer to Master Pee and asks Pee, "Have you written the music to a song of your own yet?"

Master Pee looks up and says, "Just yesterday, I finished my own creation."

Robert flashes his best smile and replies, "Would you play it for my sister?" Imagine that, my own brother using me to get Master Pee to play. It's okay this time, because I really would like to hear him play. As though greatly honored, he positions his hands over the keys, closes his eyes, and fills that empty church with one heavenly sound after another. Soon, he is singing the vocals too. His sister, Lenora, comes in just in time to join him. They sing two-part harmony. Then they take turns singing solo. Though empty, that church is filled to the top of its cross with the music that Master Pee plays.

Once satisfied, they stop singing and Master Pee stops playing. The church is as quiet as a moment of silent prayer. Master Pee turns his baby off and stands up. Though it towers over him, Master Pee is larger than life when he sends life from his fingers, onto the keys, and out of those pipes. Robert thanks him, smiles and hands me back to Master Pee. As he reaches for me, he inquires, "Baby girl, do you think it's good enough for a kiss?" Make no mistake; babies understand words like, "kisses" and "hugs." I give him two kisses and a hug. Master Pee carries me back to where Mom is waiting for us. He thanks Mom. Then, he tells her that he wants to see us again real soon. Needless to say, the feeling is mutual.

As soon as the car starts to move, I fall asleep. It is almost four o'clock, and I have missed my nap. I have sweet dreams filled with music. I was awakened by Mom taking my Sunday clothes off. I am back in my bed wondering if those wondrous things were dreams, or did they really happen?

Everyday, someone says something about that Sunday with Master Pee and his unforgettable music. Mom and Dad promise that they will take us back there soon. It won't be too soon for me!

A few weeks pass, when a card comes in the mail inviting our family back to church to a graduation party for Master Pee. This evening, Mom and Dad are going to visit Aunt Margaret and Uncle Van. Since the other kids have plans of their own, they take me with them. Dad takes the country route, because Mom wants to buy flowers for her hanging baskets. As they ride, Dad comments that Master Pee looks like his great-grandparent's Hazel and Aunt Pearla.

Mom sits silently for a long time when she says, "I can see Aunt Pearla now, singing, patting her foot to the music, and telling everyone that's my baby. Ain't he something?"

Dad smiles and says, "Quiet as it's kept, she could soft shoe better than me." Dad laughs, recalling the day when they took Aunt Pearla to watch him play ball. Dad was the star player for the Clover Stars baseball team. They were all city champions for seven years running. Aunt Pearla was not happy with Dad, because he only hit two home runs that day.

He says, "She had the nerve to say, so what happened today, Oak (as she called him)? Did I make you nervous?" Angry at himself for getting a triple, he asks, "How do you know what I hit?" She laughed then replied, "Boy, I'm blind, not deaf, in case you hadn't noticed." Then she gives him a little shove with her cane. So, Aunt Pearla was Master Pee's great-grandmother. It's no wonder he's such a nice young man, as he comes from good stock. They say Master Pee has been accepted to a college in Washington, D.C. He wants to become a mortician.

Mom looking out the window asks, "I wonder what made him decide to do that?"

We stop at the nursery. Mom gets her flowers, and we go on to Aunt Margaret and Uncle Van's house. When we arrive, they are sitting on their front porch. They live in a large white duplex on a quiet tree-lined street, with large porches and even larger yards. It seems almost everyone on their street is from the Carolinas. Whenever Mom and Dad come here, they spend most of the time talking across fences, in yards or on porches. Kids play, ride bikes, or walk from one friend's house to another.

GRADUATION DAY

I'd almost forgotten about Master Pee's graduation party. Then, one Sunday morning, I awaken to all the kids happily getting ready for church. This morning, no one asks if they have to go to church. Mom comes to get me up saying, "Wake up, sleepyhead; its time to get you ready for church. Today is Master Pee's graduation party, and he's waiting to see you again."

Robert comes into the room, bends over to kiss me, and say, "If you give Master Pee one of your kisses, maybe he will play his song for you again." Still laughing, he walks away. I think to myself, that was then; and this is now. The kids spend hours teaching me to say Master Pee's name. On the ride to church, they repeat the words they want me to say. Sunday school was already over, when we arrive. Robert takes me from Mom. He carries me over to where Master Pee is standing near his parents. Master Pee notices Robert before we reach him, and he starts walking toward us. They share hellos. Then Robert says, "I brought someone to see you!" Robert bends down and lowers me to the ground next to him. Pee looks down. Then, he bent down so that we are eye to eye.

He smiles and says, "Look who's standing! Are you too big now to give Pee a little kiss?" I reach up and put both arms around his neck. Holding me out in front of him, he stands up.

To his surprise I say, "Hi, my Pee," and kiss him on his cheek. He looks as though he is in shock. He finds his voice and then says, "Can you say that again, baby girl?" I think to myself, Can I, say it again? Okay, here we go!

"Hi, my Pee."

When I finish, he says, "You forgot the best part. Where is my kiss, baby girl?" Talking must be another milestone for babies. It receives the same reception as being a newborn, crawling, or walking. Master Pee carries me to his mother; and then, he asks me to say hello once more.

When I finish speaking, he holds me over his head, spinning me around in the air the way Robert does. They laugh and laugh. Finally, he put me down on the ground to walk me back to Mom. Master Pee asks Mom for permission to take me into church with them. Mom tells me to be a good girl; then she instructs Robert to bring me back if I become tired. Even before she finishes speaking, we are off.

The clock on the wall says it's time for church to begin. At that moment, the large oak doors open and we step inside. Everyone who comes into that vestibule speaks to, shakes hands with, congratulates, or embraces Master Pee. The minister, Reverend Washington, and the choir come through an open door. Like magic, Aunt Margaret appears dressed and ready to usher them to their seats. Looking surprised, she smiles at seeing me with Master Pee and not Mom. She gives me a kiss, so now I have lipstick on my cheek while everyone else has it on their lips. She tells Master Pee it is time to go! He replies, "We are waiting on you, Mrs. Margaret!" Master Pee picks me up and says, "Come on, baby girl, let's go make music." As he walks down that long isle, Master Pee tells me he is going to play his song today. When he reaches the top of the stairs leading to the organ, he takes my hand and we walk over to his stool. He sits me on the stool. Next, he sits down beside me. Even from here I can almost hear Mom telling me, "You be a good girl for me; do you hear!" I watch as Master Pee flips the switches that bring life to his oversized toy. I know he is ready when he places his hands high over the keys. Using one finger, he hits the same note three times. Then he raises his hands once more, just as before he becomes a one man orchestra. At a predetermined time, the choir led today by Master Pee's sister, Lenora, starts singing. They weave their voices, becoming one with the music. Nodding his head, Master Pee rocks from side to side, sometimes playing with his eyes closed as he fills those pipes with joy. Master Pee doesn't just play. He loves to play! In utter amazement, I watch him select each key, flip the switches, and push the pedals. The music is different when one is sitting on the stool next to the master player. I see music in the making, I feel it live, and I hear it up close and personal.

At the conclusion of the service, Lenora comes over to the microphone. She congratulates Master Pee for his success in graduating. She then says, "Today, my brother has added yet another first to an already long list of successful accomplishments in his short lifetime. It is my pleasure to accompany him with the vocals to a song he penned. It's called 'You Always Cared.'" He takes a deep breath, gives me a wink, and sets his fingers free. He caresses the keys, mixes sounds, makes one note bounce on the top of another note that he holds flat. He makes flutes play to harps, trumpets call a base fiddle, they join a guitar and drums that beat the sound of one man's personal prayer up through those giant pipes and out over the church. The choir and Lenora sing as though they know this is special, as though they know it doesn't get any better than this. But it did! From right beside me, Master Pee sings his song from a place where great songs are born. He gives it life, meaning, feeling, and rhythm. Then he set it free, to touch the world of those who have the pleasure of witnessing the greatness of a master player. When I look out at the congregation, I know Master Pee and that choir of angels have found a new song to touch each heart. On this Sunday he baptizes each heart, with the sound of his words set to music. On behalf of everyone, I plan to give "My Pee" a hug and this time, I won't forget to give him one of my best baby kisses.

My First Birthday

Summer follows spring, walking follows crawling, teeth come one at a time, and so with words. Now, there is a new fascination in my life. Mom says it will go on all the days of my life. "Words," it seems there are millions of them. Each day, she teaches me new ones, like "stop, no, yes, please, thank you, and why." As I'm learning to say and understand words, the kids are singing them. Today, they are teaching me to sing "Happy Birthday." They forget that I now understand what they are saying. This morning, I overheard Mom reminding them that I'm having a birthday party this afternoon.

Today is my first birthday. The party is supposed to be a surprise. They have worked so hard keeping the party a surprise. I'm going to act surprised. It's early in the morning, the kids are in school, and we are home alone. First thing this morning, Mom tells me happy birthday and gives me one of her best mommy kisses. This morning, Mom is babysitting for her friend; so, therefore, I have someone to play with. William is two years old, and he is into building blocks. Mom is baking a cake. I know it's for me, because yellow cake with coconut icing is my favorite. By noon, Mom has finished cleaning and ironing. Flowers are in their place in the living room and dining room. We are playing on the floor as she changes the curtains in my room. William's mom is back, and he has to go home for lunch. Mom tells me, now that I'm one, that I have to put my toys away. I guess that's what happens when you become one. After lunch, we walk to the store to get candles. On the way, Mom shows me how to run backward and how to skip. That was fun! We share a Popsicle on the way home. She tells me her friend, Leroy, taught her to skip and to run backward. I ask where Leroy lives.

She says, "Leroy went into the army to help fight for our freedom. He died in the war, and he lives in heaven now." She stops walking, bent down in front of me, and says, "Let me show you something else Leroy taught me." Mom then teaches me a little game called "patty cake." We play and laugh all the way home. That afternoon, she prepares my favorite meal with all the pretty colored vegetables. The best part of my birthday comes when Mom places the cake with one candle in the center of the table. They sing "Happy Birthday" to me, and I sing with them. Birthdays must be special. Robert gives me a glass of his ice tea. He then asks me for a hug like the ones I give Master Pee. Albert gives me a turtle he calls Amos. Mom says that I have to keep him in my room so that no one steps on him. Albert's favorite drink is "chocolate milk." He waits for the milkman every morning so that he can drink it before he goes to school. Sometimes I wait with him because it is really better than the milk I drink.

After we have cake and homemade ice cream, we go outside. The kids fill the balloons with water and have a balloon fight. Mom and Dad come outside to watch us play. Nobody tells me that they are off limits, so I throw water balloons at them too. Parents show no mercy on little kids. They throw balloons back at me. The kids think it is funny to see them all wet, so did I. That is even better than the birthday cake.

At the end of a perfect first birthday, I welcome the night. Its 8:30 p.m., and it's still not dark outside. I love the long days of summer. Mom has bathed me and put new pj's on me. As I sit in my chair, Mom braids my hair. Dad is sitting in a rocking chair as he listens to the Brooklyn Dodgers game. So as not to disturb him, Mom waits for the teams to change sides.

"Did I mention to you that I haven't seen my friend yet?" she says.

After a long silence, without opening his eyes he says, "So, when was the last time you saw her?"

Mom replies, "April!"

Dad opens his eyes, sits up and says, "Then you can forget her until next year." After a long silence, he says, "Maybe this should be the last time." What a strange conversation. I thought we had met all of Mom's friends. Dad picks up his cigarettes, walks downstairs, and outside. Mom finishes braiding my hair; then, she put lotion on my face and hands. We go into the kitchen to get me a glass of water. When I look out the open window, Dad is walking around in his garden as he assesses the new growth. I watch him finish smoking his cigarette; then he puts it out in the dirt at the edge of his garden. Mom tells me that it's bedtime for me. I want to say good night to Dad, so I put my face in the open window and say, "Good night, Dad."

"Stay right there, or I will miss my good-night kisses," he says as he runs up the path across the yard and jumps over the picnic table. Before I reach the top of the stairs, he is there. "So, what do I get for getting here in a flash?" We share our nightly hugs and kisses as he carries me off to bed.

Mom's Friend

Summer slides into fall and fall into winter. I never hear my parents mention Mom's friend anymore. It's Thanksgiving Day. Uncle Van and Aunt Margaret come to have dinner with us. When everyone is seated at the table, Dad blesses the food. At the end of the blessing he adds, "Thank the Lord for the joy of our baby, due in February." After dinner, while washing my face and hands, Lorraine explains, we are getting a sister or brother in February. I want to know, when is February and is it going to be a boy or a girl? She explains as best as she can.

When I continue to ask more questions, she says, "You will have to wait, just as we did for you." I, of course, have more questions, but I know she isn't going to answer them. So I let her go, for now.

Before I have forgotten Thanksgiving, Lorraine is decorating the Christmas tree again. Mom is getting bigger each day. She says that she is eating for two. Day and night exchange places, weeks turn into months. Finally, January becomes February. On the fourth night of February, as I sleep, Dad takes Mom to the hospital. That next morning, the kids are all excited. Dad had come home sometime during the night as I slept, to tell them that Mom has had a baby girl. He says the baby's name is Margaret. It seems that everything happens when I'm asleep. The next morning, I sit at the head of the stairs waiting for Dad to come home from work. Once again I have questions.

When he comes through the door, I am waiting. He smiles, picks me up, and says, "It's a girl! You have a new sister."

"Dad, where's Mom?"

He explains that Mom has to stay at the hospital until they become strong enough to come home. This is the first time I've been separated from Mom. It feels strange being home without her in the house. After a few days, I am afraid she isn't coming back. Robert and Lorraine try to assure me that Mom will come home as soon as she can. Five days seem like an eternity to me. Finally, one day, Dad comes home from work, and Mom and the baby are with him. I am so excited to see Mom that I forget all about the baby. Lorraine now almost eighteen and Ruby now eight, are already meeting Margaret.

When I finally go into Mom's room, there on the bed is a small blanket with an even smaller baby inside. She looks exactly like Mom. She opens her eyes, sees me looking at her, and from that moment, she follows me with her eyes until she is old enough to literally follow me. I will never forget that first night my little sister came home. She is so small and cute lying on Mom's bed wrapped in her little pink blanket. Up to this point, she has not made one sound. She sleeps on Mom's lap for almost an hour. Somewhere around 8:00 p.m. Mom carries her into our room. Oh yes, now I have a roommate. Did anyone ask me if I'd like someone sharing my space? No, as I explained earlier, we babies really can't say anything. Well, Mom puts that little bundle of joy down in the crib and makes that fatal mistake. She turns the light off. Even before the light is off, mamas' new baby starts screaming at the top of her lungs. Each time Mom turns the light off, baby girl opens her eyes and her mouth. After a few minutes of screaming, Mom leaves the light on and the door opened. It is quiet once more. I like this new baby already.

I see nothing has changed. The milk is back and so is that smiling baby on those little jars. I'm glad I'm around to help her avoid the pitfalls that we babies go through. I wait two or three weeks to be sure baby girl is up to something more than baby food. When Mom leaves the room, I slip her a sip of juice or tea. She loves mashed potatoes, corn flakes, crushed broccoli, and the like. I keep the family fur ball out of her face and stay up with her until she falls asleep. When she gets that my back and bottom are killing me look, I turn her over. This baby wakes up at 5:00 a.m. every morning. After she has her bottle, she goes back to sleep for three or four hours. Then, little bright eyes are up and ready to keep everybody busy. I wonder what she's thinking. I know she's not a member of the smiley-face baby food fan club. I explain the man in the moon to her, and she's all right with him now. It's one of these two afternoons when baby girl and I are in the living room on the couch. Now, six or seven months old, she wants to go wherever I go. Well, we haven't had that "crawl before you walk talk" yet. Margaret is lying on the couch, and I am jumping up and down on it, because it makes her laugh. In her excitement, she rolls to the edge. With the next roll, she goes off the couch and rolls into the middle of the floor. She looks up at me on the couch, and she starts to laugh. It is as though she has just learned to fly. That is the only time I've ever seen a flying baby. I climb off the couch down onto the floor where she lay laughing. She didn't cry, so I assume she isn't hurt. We play until she gets tired. Then, we do what we do best and go to sleep. Now, I understand what Dad meant when he said, "Maybe this should be the last one." This seems like a good place to end the game at six children. I teach her everything the bigger kids teach me. When I start school, I bring my homework home so that she can sit with me to learn as I learn. She likes learning and listening to stories. Compared to everyone else, Margaret is small and doesn't seem to be growing. She is like my shadow. When we go shopping for school clothes, she wants whatever Mom buys me. All she has to do is cry, and Mom buys it for her. So, we dress alike even before we start to school.

Just before my sixth birthday, I develop bronchitis and have to be hospitalized for three weeks. I miss Margaret more than anyone. I miss playing with her and talking under the covers until we get yelled at. I will never forget seeing her for the first time. Kids under twelve are not allowed to visit anyone at the hospital. This is the first time since she came home from the hospital that we are apart. Mom and Dad come to check me out of the hospital. It is spring. It means that it is cold in upstate New York. I walk outside the hospital holding hands with Mom and Dad. Even before we reach the car, I can see Margaret standing in the back seat with her face pressed against the window. I think she will smile at the sight of me, but she does what she always does when she's happy or sad. One giant tear rolls down her cheek and comes to rest on her chin. She looks like a walking doll dressed in her burgundy, velvet snowsuit. She is wearing the world's smallest stirrup pants and hat. Everyone remembers that first snowsuit. Dad opens the back door as Margaret moves to the middle of the seat, crawls up, and sits down. She doesn't say a word, she just looks at me the way she had the first time I ever saw her. As we start the ride home, I feel her hand touch mine. She moves her hand away. Then she touches me again as though making sure I am real. I hold her hand all the way home. No matter where I go, she holds on and watches my every move. When we put our pajamas on for bed, she starts to talk. She has questions about doctors, nurses, needles, and about why she couldn't come to visit me. Just before she goes to sleep, she says that she doesn't want me to go away again. Still holding on to my hand, she falls asleep.

This fall is special. We have taught Margaret all we know. Now it is her turn to start school. She knows her numbers, can recite the ABC's and can print. All this knowledge should have made school just another easy game. I take her to her classroom, introduce her to her teacher, and prepare to leave. She realizes that I am not staying with her, but going to my first-grade class. She starts to cry. After a sister-to-sister talk, she promises to stop crying. I wasn't in my classroom twenty minutes before her teacher sent someone to get me. This went on every morning for a week. Finally, her teacher asks me to take her to my class with me. My teacher says, "If she is going to be in my class, she will have to do first grade assignments."

That night, I explain to Mom and Dad what my teacher said. They ask Margaret what she wants to do. She smiles and says she wants to stay with me. We sit next to each other in school from that day until graduation. She was my best little friend, and she is still little and my best friend.

THE LOVE OF THE GAME

As you know, my parents are baseball people. They have their favorite teams, but they will watch other teams, when their team has a day off for travel. It is funny how the kids, though we don't listen to or watch the games instinctively, pick up things like game times, or what the score is when we go past the TV. A favorite question is, "Who's winning, and by how much? I remember keeping my dad posted with the blow by blow as he worked in the yard or on his car. If Dad comes to pick us up from school or from a friend's house, we get in the car and automatically ask, "What's the score?"

I remember their after-the-game discussions and their predictions for future games. Dad listens to the entire game, regardless of the outcome. Mom thinks if she turns it off, it will change her team's performance. When she turns it on later, she will learn her team has won. This doesn't happen often. In reality, she just cannot stand to see them lose, lose, and lose.

My sister, Lorraine, takes this love of baseball to a whole new level. She has score cards with the names of coaches, umpires, owners, players, and even batboys for each game. As soon as she is old enough, she is on every club or church bus headed to New York City to watch the Dodgers or the Giants play ball. I enjoy the emotion my parents express regarding each event in their after game playback.

It's because of their pleasure, interest and excitement that I wrote a poem that incorporates our game of life to the game of baseball. We the players hope that you enjoy our game of life as much as we have.

The Fifth Seed Winners

By Mercedes Bleu

WHEN TWO YOUNG LOVERS MARRIED,
THEY HAD NONE.
TWO YEARS LATER CAME . . . SEED NUMBER ONE.
THEIR FIRST . . . A JOYOUS BABY GIRL!
SOMEONE UNIQUELY THEIRS TO SHARE WITH THE WORLD.
FOUR YEARS LATER, A NEW SEED GREW;
PLEASE WELCOME SEED NUMBER TWO!
THEIR FIRST BORN SON . . .
AND THE SCORE WAS ONE TO ONE.
FOUR YEARS LATER, THE GAME OF LIFE
WAS PLAYED AGAIN.
SEED NUMBER THREE THEIR SECOND SON, CAME IN,
AND THE SCORE WAS TWO TO ONE
FOUR YEARS PASSED, AND AGAIN THE GAME WAS PLAYED.
SEED NUMBER FOUR, A BABY GIRL
WITH LOVING CARE, SEED ONE, TWO, THREE, AND FOUR
DID WHAT SEEDS DO, THEY GREW!
THE SCORE WAS TIED AT TWO AND TWO;
THE FIFTH SEED, THE TIE BREAKER WAS DUE
FOR THE SEEDS WHO CAME BEFORE
THEY "THANK YOU" MOMMY AND DADDY
FOR PLAYING THE GAME OF LIFE.
MOST OF ALL, I THANK YOU.
"YES," FOUR YEARS WENT BY.

IT WAS JUNE AND THE SUN WAS HIGH,
WHEN THE DOOR OF LIFE OPENED,
THE FIFTH SEED, A GIRL ARRIVED.
I WAS THAT FIFTH SEED
FOR TWO YEARS, THE SCORE STOOD AT TWO TO THREE.
FEBRUARY, THE SIXTH SEED, WHAT WOULD IT BE?
A BOUNCING BABY GIRL SLID THROUGH
FINAL SCORE FOUR TO TWO,
AND THE GIRLS WIN

A Winter Wonderland

Though only sixty miles apart, Albany is a whole world away from Kingston when it comes to the weather. Those beautiful mountains and the Hudson River can take a storm that dumps ten to twelve inches of snow in Albany and turn it into a blizzard in the Hudson Valley.

I remember one such storm blew into the valley one Christmas Eve. Ten or twelve inches of snowfall, which made this Christmas poster perfect. The kids are everywhere enjoying their snowball fights, making snowmen, and sleigh riding off every hill they could find. Since they are on vacation, they spent all day playing in that stuff called snow.

The world is a quiet place when snow cover muffles the otherwise noticeable sounds of car engines, horns, and church bells. Everyone goes to sleep that night with sidewalks and driveways plowed and ready for Christmas. That Sunday night, a snowstorm comes down the Hudson Valley, and by sunrise, more than twenty-five inches of snow had fallen. When the storm tries to retreat over the river, the tide comes in and pushed that snowstorm back into the valley. It snows continuously all that second day and night. By the morning of the third day, almost four feet of snow has fallen.

After breakfast, everyone goes outside to shovel snow. Mom makes hot chocolate, coffee, and tea that she brings outside every few hours.

Whole families spend that day shoveling a path out of their homes. When the plows finally shovel the streets, it is like a maze. When I walk in the street and my sister walks on the sidewalk, we are unable to see each other until we come to a street corner. We climb up on top of the four to six foot banks of snow to watch people walking on the streets below.

Most people cannot get their cars out of the snow, even if they want to. Each of my brothers has his own sleigh. Since Dad can't get the car out of the garage, my brothers go to the bus stop to pick up Mom. They take two blankets and two straps with them. They wrap her in the blankets and strap her to the sleigh to pull her home. Knowing she can't stop them, they run up and down the high banks of snow. She enjoys the ride, even though she threatens to skin them if she lives through it. The next morning, they ride her back to the bus stop and promise to be there waiting when she gets off the bus.

By the evening of the third day, people and snow plows have cleaned the streets, driveways, and sidewalks. My brothers take us with them to pick Mom up this evening. Robert pulls Ruby on his sled, and Albert pulls me. They don't just pull you along the smooth flat path; they go up on top of the four foot mounds of snow and then run down the other side. The more we scream, the more they do to make us scream.

Wearing gloves, boots, hat, and ear muffs, Mom is dressed for a blizzard. When we start for home, Robert is pulling Mom, and Albert has Ruby and me on his sleigh. First, they decide to race. They soon get tired and have to rest. During the rest period a snowball fight ensues. The high banks of snow make a great barrier between the teams. Finally, my brothers rush the snow wall, and we surrender.

Mom says, "They should be ashamed for cheating a couple of kids and a defenseless woman." She vows to make them pay. She threatens not to fix dinner that evening. I can still see Robert wiping the splattered snow off her coat and hat. He offers her a ride the rest of the way home. She laughs telling him he might want to save his strength, especially since he will not be having any dinner. After a few minutes of teasing them, Albert and Mom pull Robert home. Mom is always thinking. After dinner, she asks Robert to set the trash outside for her. Robert has a habit of grabbing his hat and coat and sticking his bare feet into the rubber boots. As he is eating dinner, Mom is filling his boots with snow. When he sticks his bare feet in his boots, he grows two or three feet in that moment. This is the first time I've seen him dance. It looks as though his feet are stuck in his boots. The more he tries to get them off, the more they hang on. Mom gets her laugh on watching Robert jump up to avoid the snow, though he knows that when he comes down, it will be there waiting for him. As he dances, he swears to get even with whoever put snow in his boots. When his head and heart return to normal, he realizes all the kids are at the table eating dinner with him. When he looks at Mom, she is laughing uncontrollably. He knows she is guilty of giving him cold feet. Mom tells Robert the cold snow brings out the Indian in him. She asks him to do his snow dance again. Robert has that "I will get you back look" in his eye. Mom suggests he laugh it off and remember to be nicer to those who brought him into this world. After his feet thaw, he is back laughing and playing with Mom.

Mom announces on Saturday that Dad's sister, her husband, and their two kids are coming to Sunday dinner. That means Mom will be baking pies for dessert. On Sunday, our uncle, aunt, and our two cousins come to dinner. Just before dinner is finished, Mom excuses herself from the table saying she has to take her pies out of the oven. Our kitchen is on the second floor. Mom always opens the kitchen window a few inches and sets her pies there to cool. She returns to the table and goes back to talk and eat. Saying that they have to go the bathroom, Robert and Albert excuse themselves from the table.

They go downstairs as though going to the bathroom. Next, they put their coats, boots, and gloves on, go outside, get Dad's ladder, and put it up to the kitchen window. Albert holds the ladder as Robert climbs up to take Mom's still steaming pies and brings them down to Albert. They put her pies on the coffee table in the living room on the first floor. The kids return the ladder, come inside, take off their coats and boots, and then return to the table. When dinner is over, the dishes and food are cleared from the table. Mom announces she has made apple and lemon pies for dessert. As always, the boys get dishes and silverware to put on the table. Mom gets up saying she doesn't want them to drop her lemon pies. Lemon pie is Dad's favorite dessert. He is sitting at the table with fork in hand. When he can wait no more, he says, "If talk and pies were one and the same, that lemon pie would already be in my digestive track." Mom walks over to the kitchen window. Then, she reaches to grab her three waiting pies. She finds only a partially opened window. Retracing in her mind placing those three pies in that window, she stands there in disbelief. Now, not sure she had placed them there at all, she walks over to the stove and opens the oven. Up to this point, she hasn't said a word. Realizing the desserts are not in the oven or on the windowsill, she walks over to the window, raises it, and looks down to see if they have fallen.

Now, totally confused she say, "Olen, did you move the pies from the windowsill?"

"Stop playing, woman; I've waited all day for that lemon pie; so, bring it on," he says. Mom is not happy. She has guest! Dad wants his pie, but Mama's famous pies have vanished. After an exhausting search of the kitchen, Dad says, "Maybe you only thought you made those pies?" Everyone is making light of the missing pies, but Mom is just one block from mad.

Dad suggests the adults retire to the living room so that the kids can clean the kitchen. They are joking about the missing pies, as Mom is looking at the apple peelings, cores, and boxes of lemon mix. She knows she made pies. Reluctantly, she takes her coffee and follows Dad along with my aunt and uncle downstairs to our living room. When they enter the living room, there on the coffee table are Mom's three pies. Dad and Uncle Ray see the pies and comment. "Cynthia, you only thought you put them in the window," says Uncle Ray. They tease her about losing her memory and about forgetting where she put the pies. Mom knows she would never set hot pie pans on her coffee table. She gets up, goes into the boy's room, opens the window, and looks out. There in the fresh snow are footprints and holes in the snow from the ladder. She comes back in the hall where she finds the boys wet boots and gloves. Then she goes back into the living room to tell everyone what her boys have done. Now, the game is on. They decide to play a game with the boys. Dad's heart just is not in the game. He has waited too long for his piece of pie. But, Mom convinces him to go along with her scheme.

She goes into the hall closet, opens the cooler to place her pies inside. From the bottom of the stairs, she calls Robert to bring her some sugar for her coffee. Robert has been looking for an excuse to come downstairs since Mom has not mentioned finding her pies.

He grabs the sugar bowl from the table and almost runs down the stairs. When he enters the living room, there are no pies and no one mentions finding them. Robert has that same confused look on his face that Mom had when her pies weren't on the windowsill. Finally, he gets up the courage to ask Mom when the kids can have dessert. Mom replies, "You will have to give them cookies and ice cream because I forgot to make pies today." She promises him she will make pies tomorrow. Robert wants to confess now, but he doesn't know where the pies are. His plan has backfired. Confused, he excuses himself and leaves the room. Robert now realizes he is in a world of trouble. It's time he tells his partner in crime, Mama's baby boy, Albert, that the elusive pies are no longer on the coffee table. At this point, Albert wants to confess, but he changes his mind when Robert asks him what he will say when Dad asks him what they did with the pies. Albert is a quiet shy boy who never gets in trouble, and he really doesn't want any trouble now. Mom knows that Robert talked Albert into helping him with this scheme. In her calm quiet manner, she has Albert bring her purse downstairs. Robert, now back upstairs, follows Albert into Mom's room to instruct him not to tell her that they took her pies. Now, Albert has had enough of this missing pie dilemma.

For the first time, he steps up to Robert and says, "I don't know anything about any pies. All I did was hold the ladder for you. So, stop talking to me about the pies that won't stay where you put them. Now, get out of the way so that I can take Mom her pocketbook." As he walks toward the stairs, he mumbles, "From now on, don't ask me to help with anymore of your brilliant schemes." By the time Albert enters the living room, he is so angry that he is puffed-up like a pregnant toad. The look on his face, as he stands by the arm of the couch, is the perfect opportunity for Mom to ask him what is wrong? As she speaks, she takes a pack of juicy fruit gum from her purse. Albert loves gum. She would buy packs of gum just for him. On this occasion, she takes one stick of gum out of the pack, put it in her mouth, and then drops the pack back into her purse. Albert, wanting his sugar fix, asks her for a stick of gum. Mom has her answer waiting for him.

Without taking a breath, she replies, "You mean you want more sweets? Didn't you just finish eating three pies?" Angry and hurt, Albert tells the whole story. At this point, he is considering crying in front of company. Mom takes his hand and walks him over to the closet. She opens it; then she asks him to take the cooler upstairs for her. He carries the cooler upstairs and sets it on a chair. Robert is not happy with himself or Albert, but he is busy concentrating on avoiding Mom. She lets him suffer for a few minutes more before clearing up the matter of her famous missing pies.

She walks over to him, places her hand on his shoulder; and says, "Do you think you can do something for me? Please! Could you take my pies out of that cooler, cut them into slices, put them on plates, and then, give one slice to everyone. Let's see if they can lose it in their mouths. Boy, your dad isn't laughing; so, I suggest you start serving downstairs first." Relieved that he can keep his skin, Robert opens the cooler. He couldn't help but smile at the sight of Mom's pies.

When he cuts the lemon pie, he makes sure to give Dad a large slice. Now he has to take it to him. As Robert carries the slices of pie across the kitchen, Albert still angry says, "I hope you stumble and drop that pie on Daddy; so, he can kill you." Robert doesn't have time to reply. He is now concentrating on not dropping those elusive slices of pie. He serves the ladies first. Then he turns to serve Dad.

Dad waits until Robert extends the pie when he says, "I thought I might have to turn you upside down to shake this pie out of you. Boy, please go give those kids their pie before they beat you up."

Robert tries to get Mom to tell him how she knew that he took her pies. She laughs and then tells him, "I know my babies."

One day, weeks later, Mom and Dad go to visit one of their friends in the hospital. They leave me home with Robert. Robert could spend an entire day reading comic books. After a few hours, I get bored. I go to his room to ask him to walk me to the store to get a Popsicle. I know he is going to say no; nevertheless, I am ready for him. I stick my head in the opened door of his room and state, "I know what happened to those pies you lost, and I know how Mom knew you took them." I tell him that I heard Mom tell our neighbor Ida the whole story." He tries to bribe me with a dime, which I take. I tell him that now I have a dime all I need is a Popsicle. Finally, his curiosity gets the better of him. He rides me to the store on his bicycle. When we get home, we share my strawberry Popsicle. As we sit on the front steps, I tell him how he got caught. When I'm finish telling him the whole story, we finish our Popsicle. Robert has to laugh, because he realizes he is no match for Mom. He's back in his room reading comic books, but I'm sure he's working on another one of his famous schemes.

MAMA'S BABY BOY

My younger brother Albert is sixteen years old and mentally sure he can drive. He has not driven a car alone or with supervision, yet he asks Dad almost daily for the opportunity to take the car out of the garage. He continues asking the same question over and over for weeks. It is late in the afternoon, just after dinner when we are all gathered in the kitchen. Dad says that he is going to the service station to fill the car with gas. As always, Albert asks Dad to let him take the car out of the garage. I don't know if he is tired of the same question or what, but this time is different. Dad turns around, looks him in the eyes, and says, "Boy, you are determined to do this. So, go ahead." With a sigh of relief, he hands Albert the keys to the car. Fearing Dad might change his mind, Albert takes the keys, runs down the stairs, outside, across the porch, and around to the garage. Mom and I are looking out the kitchen window. From where we are standing, we are looking down on the garage. Albert flings the garage door open and then jumps into the car. He starts the car, puts it in reverse, and floors the accelerator. Dad's shiny black Olds bolts out of the garage. The speed panics my brother, who proceeds to turn the steering wheel as far to the left as he can. He comes around the corner of the house going twenty-five or thirty miles per hour, hit the porch, and wipes it out.

The impact of the car hitting the porch shakes the house, rattles every dish and glass in Moms' china closet and then sends shock waves through every window in the house. There in the driver's seat sits my brother Albert. He is now terrified that Dad is going to kill him. He looks as though he is in shock. When the house stops shaking, Dad walks over to the window next to Mom and says, "Tell me that boy didn't run into the house." Slowly, he walks down the stairs. Nobody says a word. He jumps down to the ground, walks over to the car, and opens the door. Even in shock, Albert knows this meant "get out." Without a word, he jumps out of the still running car and runs to his room. Dad moves the car away from the porch to park it in the driveway. Talking to himself, Dad gets out of the car. He mumbles, "How do you tear down a porch and not put a scratch on the car?"

When I look up at Mom, she has that grin on her face that means I wish I could laugh, because it really is a funny sight. Still in disbelief, Dad gets in his car and goes to get gas. He isn't twenty feet away from the house before Mom says, "Did you see that?" Then, she starts to laugh until tears stream down her cheeks. She says, "The look on Dad's face was exactly the same as the one on Albert's face." Dad is almost normal when he comes home.

We watch Dad walk down the hall to my brother's room, open the door and say, "Boy, meet me outside tomorrow at one o'clock. We have a porch that needs repair, and when we are finished, I'm going to teach you how to drive."

Early the next morning, Mom is outside. When I wake up, she is watering her plants. Ida, our next-door neighbor, comes out of her house and over to where Mom is standing. Through the open window, I hear her ask Mom, "How is Albert? I hear he ran Oak's car into the porch? So, tell me what hospital is he in?" They laugh and laugh some more. They laugh at Albert, then at Dad for hours. Mom says her sides hurt from laughing so much. Mom tells Ida that Albert didn't get a whipping for the porch, but had he broken her china, he wouldn't be able to sit for days. To make up for ripping the porch down, Albert becomes the best driver I've ever known.

Albert graduates high school that next June and starts looking for a summer job. In early July, he comes home happier than he has been in months. He looks as though he has all the answers. A-g-a-i-n! He catches Mom preparing dinner alone in the kitchen. He tells her he has found the job he has been searching for. He goes on to explain that he needs her signature to accept the job because his eighteenth birthday is three months away. The job of his choice is the United States Marine Corps. Enlistees must be eighteen years old or have parental consent. Though he has a shy, quiet boyish manner, he is six feet tall. All through high school, he plays in the school band, and he is handsome in his uniform. Albert is Mama's baby boy, who not only wants to move out, but he wants to put himself in harm's way. I'm sure she is proud of his choice. She just isn't ready for change today. Just as he had done when he wanted to take the car out of the garage, Albert is relentless about her signature that he needs to enlist in the Marine Corps. Mom and Dad discuss his decision when the kids are asleep. Since his birthday is fast approaching, they reluctantly sign the papers. Albert's best friend and next-door neighbor, Cameron, is already eighteen. They plan to enlist under the buddy plan. They take the test together, and they both pass it. Within weeks, they are off to basic training.

Albert writes Mom letters twice a week. She reads them and shares his experiences with us. In the evening, she finds a quiet place just for the two of them, where she writes until she is satisfied. On my way to school, I stop at the post office to mail her letters. Each time Mr. Lasher looks over his bifocals and says, "Give this to your mom and tell her hello for me." I know Mom will be reading and writing tonight.

One night, a few months after Albert left for basic training, Mom announces that he will be coming home soon. Up to this point, I don't remember having seen a real live marine. Today, a picture of Albert in his dress blues comes with his letter. Dress blues are earned and worn on special occasions like graduation, parades, and promotion ceremonies. I look at that picture a hundred times between that day and the day he comes home. My brother Albert left home all arms and legs. He returns as Albert the marine, who is a clean-shaven young man with muscles, a great haircut, and a strong smile. He is as a clean as a new quarter! The gold ropes, stripes, and bars make him even more handsome. He no longer looks like mama's baby boy. I can't wait to see my brother, the man.

One Friday night, the front door opens and like always, Albert runs up the stairs taking them two at a time. He comes around the corner and steps to attention in our kitchen. For what seems like an eternity no one says a word. In that moment, I don't know if he even knew anyone other than Mom is in the room. Taking two giant steps, he is in front of her. In one motion, he sweeps her off her feet. He kisses her and spins her around and around in circles. Finally, he gently put her feet back on the floor. As though dizzy, she hangs on to his arms. He takes her hands in his and takes one step backward and says, "Hi, Mom . . . will I do?"

She shakes her head approvingly and replies, "You are a sight for sore eyes!" The moment of quiet shock is over. It's now hugs, kisses, and tears of joy time. He gives Dad a hug; then he picks Margaret up and dances around with her in his arms. He looks down at me, takes his hat off, and places it on my head. He gives Margaret another hug and kiss, as he places her on Mom's lap, and turns to me. As though he knows how I need to grow, he put his hands under my arms and pitches me up in the air over his head. It is as though he never left. Mom is still telling him not to throw me up in the air. Worried that I might drop his new hat, I hold on to it with both hands because I trust him to hold on to me. After a hug and kiss, he put me back to my original height. Before that moment, I never realize how tall he is, or how short I am. For the next ten days, I ride around on his shoulders. That's my idea of real growth. I've been looking up to him ever since, and that's as it should be.

Mom walks on clouds for the next ten days. All of her babies are in the nest once again. She shows him off at church, to the neighbors, and to anyone she can capture for a moment. They laugh and talk for hours. Knowing he is safe in her care, Mom seems calm and at peace. It is good to see her look approvingly at him as he talks to or plays with one of the kids. She was truly proud of whom he had become. For the next two years, he would come home bigger and better each time.

The Korean War starts, and he is off to battle. He writes Mom when time permits. This is not his favorite part of being a marine. I know he does whatever is necessary to get beyond these days because one Saturday morning our front door opens, and he is home once more. Mom thanks her friend, "the big guy." She has been walking on air ever since.

By the way, Albert's best friend, Cameron, goes to Japan when Albert ships out for Korea. He comes home four days before Albert, and they are just as they always were friends and neighbors!

THE DAY LINE

On these lazy sunny afternoons of summer, we play ball, ride our bikes, and listen to music. Mom helps Dad in his garden, or they sit in the shade of an old weeping willow, as they listen to the ball game.

The river to the east and the mountains to the west make this a picture perfect setting for home. After Sunday dinner, they walk as we run and play in the fields of lush green grass. We run along narrow paths to the road that leads to the Hudson River. We always make sure our walks start early enough to allow for playtime. We reach our favorite spot high on a hill that overlooks the south bend in the river. From this point, the view is spectacular. The river itself is breathtaking. The addition of endless trees of every size, shape, and age accents the east and west banks of the river. Beautiful wild flowers of every pastel imaginable live between the trees and jagged edge of the river. The cloudless crystal-clear blue skies of summer enhance this near-prefect setting. On days like this, the summer sun brings warmth that radiates in the air; then, it reflects the blue of the sky onto the calm water.

Every Sunday, from July to September, the most beautiful day cruise ship called the *Day Line* come up the Hudson River. She wears a fresh coat of white paint; her steel and chrome trim are polished giving her that new look. It is as though the river, calm and shimmering in the afternoon sun, waits gracefully for the thrill of having this grand lady excite her surface with wave after breaking wave. Both people and nature take a break from their routines to witness the beauty of this moment. Every Sunday, she is filled with local people and tourist enjoying the river and its view.

Each time that *Day Line* rounds that bend in the river and starts its two mile run past our house, I say, "Someday I'm going to take my parents on this ship just to see home from the river." Watching her grow larger and larger as she draws nearer is exhilarating.

These lucky travelers have the privilege of seeing the historic homes, estates, parks, and summer homes that adorn the landscape of the Hudson Valley. No Sunday would be complete without the thrill of life and beauty moving down that river.

As she passes in front of our view point, the reflection of the *Day Line* on the calm clear water keeps every eye busy moving back and forth between her reflection and her reality. They are unforgettable and exciting to everyone who bares witness. As she slips away from us, it seems as though someone is turning the volume down. The voices, the laughter, and the music fade until all is quiet once more. She grows smaller and smaller in the distance and all too soon disappears around the north bend in the river.

Two hours later, that lovely lady in white would return looking like a bride wearing a new white wedding gown. The captain and crew are her attendants and the happy tourist her wedding party. The sound of voices, laughter, and music fill the air as she passes in front of us. She rides low in the deepest channel of the river under the weight of her passengers. She almost seems to stand still for a moment. The reflection of the *Day Line* on the water is so clear that even the facial images of the travelers are clearly visible. The sight of her flags flying high and the friendly sound of her horn signal her retreat. When she is barely visible and only the splashing of her waves is all that remain, our eyes, hearts, and minds process these images, and we file them under unforgettable. She gracefully slips out of our view along the south bend in the river.

Knowing she will return in all her mesmerizing beauty come next Sunday, we are happy. Mom doesn't care much for water or boats, but she always appreciates the beauty of the *Day Line.* As it slips out of view, she says, "Now that's a sight for sore eyes." And, I agree!

On the way home sometime, Mom and Dad race us to a particular place. I know now that they let us win, but then I truly believed I could out run them both. That summer, Dad's mother, Grandma Liza, comes to visit. On this particular day, she walks with us to see *The Day Line.* We are teasing Mom and Dad because we won the race. Grandma Liza is eighty-something years old going on sixty. Being a wise old woman, she challenges me to a race. Thinking she is like my parents, I accept. Then she set the rules. She can give me a whipping with a switch, if she can catch me. I think she is crazy, when in reality I am the one having the problem. She isn't planning to win the race, she plans to do her whipping in the first four or five steps. I learn a painful lesson from that mean-spirited woman this day. After she accomplishes her mission, she tells me I should never underestimate my opponent based on age or size without taking her wisdom into consideration. I still remember waving goodbye to her when she left to return to North Carolina. The next Sunday, we are back running to see the *Day Line* come up the river and playing fair.

It's Monday morning. I hear Mom and our neighbor outside my window laughing and talking. They know a million funny stories. I'm sure Mom's sides will be hurting, when they finish laughing at the crazy things we do. By the way, Mom tells Grandma Liza that in the future if I need a whipping, she will give it to me herself. Mom tells her I didn't do anything to deserve that whipping. That summer when Mom takes the kids to visit Grandma Liza, I stay at home with Dad. Mom and her friend, Ida, are discussing my decision to stay home. Mom tells her that Dad says, I don't have to go anywhere except to school and home. Yeah!

A Moving Lesson

As a little girl, I go everywhere with my dad. I really like his car. I sit in the front seat and watch his every move. Unlike my brother, I am going to get Dad to teach me to drive. Somewhere around age seven or eight, I start using pillows on the seat to make me tall enough to see through the steering wheel. While the car sits in the driveway, I pretend I am driving. Dad walks by the car and asks me where I am going today. I pretend to be him saying that I'm going to work, to the post office, to pick up the kids, or to fish. After a month of this imaginary driving, I ask Dad to let me drive home from the store. I think he will laugh. Instead, he reaches over the seat, picks up my pillow, and places them on his lap. I sit on the pillows, while I do the steering, and he pushes the pedals. I wait for him to come home by the gate that leads into our private lane. He teaches me to steer, turn around, and park. Weeks before my tenth birthday, he let me push the pedals for the first time. First, I learn how to apply the brakes and then the accelerator. On the way home on the fourteen of June, Dad asks me what I want for my birthday. I have only one wish. I want to drive like Dad but not on his lap. I want to do it all on my own.

Dad and Ida's husband, George, work at the same place, so they take turns driving to work. This means Dad's car is at home for a whole week. Every day I wash the car. I can't wash the tires without moving the car, because the skirts covers half of the back tires. That day, while at gas station, the woman who owns the station teases Dad because half of his back tires are clean and the other half are dirty. On the way home I explain that I couldn't reach the other half of the tire without moving the car. After a long pause, he says, "You know where my keys are, and you know how to move the car." I spend hours moving the car back and forth.

Mom doesn't drive, and she doesn't have anything to do with Dad's car. One day, she comes out of the house to explain that if I do anything to the car, I will be in big trouble. On my birthday, Dad and I go to the store. I have all but given up on driving. When we turn into the lane, he stops the car; and then, he starts moving again. He says that he hears a noise in the wheel. He gets out of the car to walk around the passenger's side. He opens the door, reaches over the seat to get my pillows out of the back seat, and places them under the steering wheel. He goes back to the driver's side and adjusts the seat, so that I can reach the pedals. He closes the door to return back to the passenger side of the car. At this point, I wonder if he is showing me how to adjust the seat or if it is my time to show him what I know. In a flash, everything I have practiced for weeks vanishes from my mind. In the future, I must be more careful what I ask for. He opens my door and says, "Well! Your mother is waiting. We can't sit here all night." With that said, I slide under the steering wheel and await further instructions. He looks at me, smiles, and says, "Your mother tells me you drive, so take me home." In all of my excitement, I don't remember that drive home. I do recall that it is the greatest birthday present I ever received. Every time I drive, it reminds me of that first time in Dad's shiny black Oldsmobile.

Though Mom never has anything to do with me, Dad, and his car, she has everything to do with my first drive. In the weeks that follow, I drive up and down that lane before washing the car. Almost every day, Mom comes outside, smiles, and says, "On one of your many trips, could you go to the post office or to the store for me?" It is great being the only ten-year-old kid who has a car and parental consent to drive. Parents are great people, especially when one learns her lessons.

FAITH REWARDED

When I was a little girl, family living was the norm. Families would eat together, read, play, and pray together. Mom would tell me stories, when were alone in the kitchen. The stories she shares with me are of her experiences with her family and those she loves. As her fifth seed, I enjoy the stories we share so much that I decide to share them with you. These are only a few of the hundreds of experiences that she shared.

I seriously believe my mom improves her limited education by reading catalogs such as *Sears & Roebuck*. Back in the day, that's the way it looked. When my mom was a young girl, *Sears*, as we call it now, was a catalog store based out of Chicago. That is worlds away from Gastonia, North Carolina. I'm going to Chicago, that is, unless Oprah moves Harpo Productions to another spot. Anyway, back to Mom. She could read better than I by the time I reach junior high school. Let me introduce you to Mom's best friend. If I say, "Mom, are you going to bake a sweet potato pie tomorrow?" Her response is, "If I live and the Lord (her best friend) spares me to see tomorrow, I will make that pie." My mother loves the Lord. For he is her mother, her father, her sister, brother, and her best friend. She is humble and thankful before him, and he rewards her by allowing her to stay here almost three times as long as Jesus walked his Father's land.

Let me keep you current. On Friday, September 13, of my fourteenth year, at 3:30 a.m., my dad suffers a massive heart attack. When the sun rises that morning, he lives here no more. At this time, Ruby is eighteen and a graduating senior. Margaret and I are starting ninth grade as twelve- and fourteen-year-old teenagers.

Mom is fifty-one and fine. We have money but have big problems findings an apartment. Families live in half of their two family homes and rent the other one. The wives of men who rent have a problem with renting to three teenage girls and my fifty-one-year-young mom. Forget the numbers. We are three country kids with their mom. Soon after my dad dies, Mom has a nervous breakdown, probably shock. One week after the funeral, we become city kids. More shock! There are thousands of kids in the city school and less than one hundred in the country school. Country means grass, trees, stars, water, and more space than people. These things one doesn't see much of in the city.

I recall one quiet Saturday at home with Mom, Ruby, and Margaret. That day, Mom asks us for our opinion. Her question to us is, "How would we feel about her having a male friend or remarrying?" I remember my sisters remain sane. They aren't happy about change in our family, yet they do not voice their opinions. That day, I express my fears for the future if Mom remarries. We are safe and secure. There is peace and freedom with no man living with us. I have no idea that Mom will honor our wishes "for life." Sadly, I never see a man in our house ever.

Only after we graduate from high school, after my sisters marry and move on do I realize that we must always be careful what we ask for, because God has a sense of humor.

I still regret the things I said that day. Remember, we pay for what we say sometimes for life. To a child of fourteen, fifty is old. Now, I realize it is the perfect time for a new beginning.

We are kids unaware of adults and their issues. As for Mom, she never has another relationship after my father dies. She has the greatest respect for herself, thereby respecting us. When I have the choice to be a mother or not to be a mother, I decline. I ask myself if I can be as good as my teacher. Well, even the thought of it boggles the mind.

Long after wise women opt not to have babies I still don't have the nerve to take on the mental challenge of such an awesome responsibility. At seventeen, my mother could cook. I was forty-five when I first had to. Why would I want to settle for second best when I lived at home with the women for whom pots hum. Every chicken she kills dies for a good cause. Hamhocks, turnip greens, collards, mustard greens are health food. Mom can make greens "good!" It takes me years to know I like them. Kids truly deserve someone better than me in the kitchen.

What I'm saying is that my mother lives, learns, and loves in her faith. She works hard and is always willing to do more. She never says, "I will try." She just does what she has to do, and because she is proud, she always does her best.

Uniquely Mom

As young children, we spend almost all of our time with our mothers; therefore, we learn our mannerisms by mimicking their words and/or actions. Over the years, we amass a mental file of things Mama says, does, likes, or dislikes. Most of these qualities or habits we take on as our own.

In every child's life there is one thing our mothers do that are truly special. It's these acts or gestures that we forever hold dear. Hopefully, your memory is as pleasing and unique to you as my choice memory is to me.

I recall as a very young child learning that crying would get my mother's attention. Since it was my only means of communication, I mastered and used the art of crying whenever necessary. I must admit that I also used it selfishly, too. I have never been more thankful for the gift of vision than I am each time I see my mother as she approaches me. As I grew older, I became secure in the knowledge that though she left my visual presence, she would always be just a cry or word away. Now, beyond the crying stage, each time she leaves the room, I watch her walk away from me, too.

There was something special about her walk. As Dad would say when sharing with me the story of the day he met Mom. He recalls that she was special. He pauses then continues, saying, "As I remember, it was watching her walk away at the end of our first conversation that is still fresh in my memory." Slowly, so as not to omit one small detail, he continues, "Your mother can pop a skirt!"

"Dad, what is 'pop a skirt'?"

Your mother has a switch in her walk that makes even a simple sundress dance across the back of her legs. The hem of her dress curls around, and the momentum causes a wave in her dress to run into itself; then it comes back to meet her next step, which causes her skirt to pop. I liken it to snapping your fingers," he says. "You never lose the ability to do it. It just happens slower as one ages." He laughs out loud as though he is watching that first meeting and enjoying it once more. A slick smile replaces a pleasant grin as he continues, "When it comes to popping a skirt, it's not the speed; it's the continuous grace of motion repeated with each step that catches one's eye and holds it.

I know this is not something I should attempt to master. So, I marvel each time I witness what comes natural to her. I recall seeing her walk on Main Street or through tall grass, and it is always the same. I have not seen another lady with the ability to duplicate this simple but beautiful motion. "Popping a skirt is an enjoyable visual art."

Hot Buttered Biscuits

Mom is standing at the kitchen table. It is filled with several ingredients that alone are meaningless. She adds a cup of flour, a pinch of salt, a dash of baking powder, just the right amount of shortening and water to her liking. She applies just the right pressure and speed as she kneads, rolls, and flours the ingredients into a mass that almost resembles a ball. Next, she pulls it into two pieces, flours her dough board, and rolls her mixture into a thickness of less than one half inch. She selects a stainless steel circle cutter and begins at the edge making perfect three-inch circles. She brings her circular pan, already greased and shining, to receive her waiting circles. Mom places them in just the right position so that all eight circles fit in the pan. Using a fork, she pokes two sets of holes in each circle. She then opens a heated oven and gently slides the pan into the heat. I am always amazed at how she assembles the ingredients as well as blends and kneads the dough in less time than it takes for that dough to bake into Mama's famous hot buttered biscuits.

Mom does this while listening to me, listening to a ball game on the radio, and answering each and everyone of my sister's questions. The doorbell, telephone, and my brother's music do not distract her from finishing just another task in her kitchen. She's not preparing a meal. Mama's baby has shown her a picture of Pillsbury biscuits in a book. So, she is making us hot biscuits with melting butter sliding over their tops to their sides and down onto the saucer. There is nothing more beautiful to her than five empty plates that once held her hot buttered biscuits.

She takes the now-empty plates and jelly away, cleans up our mess, and says that we need to get out of her kitchen so she can start the dinner. Quick as a flash of lightning, we are out of her hair.

I love both my mother and my dad, and I haven't met two other people I would exchange them for. In my prayers, I always thank God for the part of them that they shared to make their fifth seed. Mama tells me how much she enjoyed school. She says playing a schoolteacher was her favorite role, as she loves to read and learn about history, the arts, sports, or flowers. As a little girl, she imagined the faraway places she had seen in magazines. She memorized states, presidents, past and present, and foreign leaders. Mom's life long dream was to become a schoolteacher. She never became one, but she became the greatest home schoolteacher we kids ever knew.

Never as a child or as an adult have I ever seen my mother dance. I do recall hearing her sing or hum in the kitchen. Mom has a way of talking with each of us. She answers our questions, and all though the other kids are in the room, they are not a part of this conservation. *When she is talking to you, you feel special; when she is talking to someone else, you never feel excluded.* It is rare to hear her raise her voice, swear, or become angry. She tells jokes, laughs, and plays. I always feel better when I leave her, than I did when I come to her.

I am grown up and out on my own before I realize that like me, each of my sisters and brothers talk to or see her almost on a daily basis. Because she sleeps best between 5:00 a.m. and 10:00 a.m., I call her every day at noon. All the other kids schedule telephone time and visiting schedules too. Home is truly where the heart is and where the love is!

THINGS MAMA SAID

1. A long little beats a short lot: To earn a large salary for a short time is not as beneficial as earning less over a lifetime. To save a little for life equals a lot.
2. Once is enough: Pray a prayer once. God will remember long after the person has forgotten.
3. No: "No" is a powerful choice that must be used. It makes one appreciate "yes."
4. Reward and punishment: To reward a child though he misbehaves, is a disservice to the child. Punishing shows the bad side of good.
5. Respect: You may choose not to love me, but you will respect me. Who should a child respect, if he is not taught by you to respect you?
6. Having children: Don't have any more children than you are prepared to work, love, and care for (for life).
7. Sex outside marriage: Why pay for life for something you can get free.
8. The do unto rule: If they aren't doing anything to you, do something for them (leave them alone).
9. Work: Work builds physical and mental muscles needed to support a person.
10. Longevity: Take life sure and easy as though it were a long trip and hope you have enough fuel to go all the way.
11. Laughter: Do it every day, and do it in a big way.
12. Arguments: Say, "I don't feel like arguing today" and walk away. It takes all the anger out of the opponent.
13. The chips don't fall far from the stump: Watch a child grow up and see how much like their roots they become.

14. Envy: Never envy what anyone has. Be grateful he shows you it's available and possible for you too.

15. Arthur and Burt: I asked Mom how she was doing. Her reply was, "Arthur and Burt are giving me fits today." "Who are Arthur and Burt?" was my question. Her answer was "Arthritis and bursitis."

Sweet Lorraine

Lorraine is twenty-one, and she has been talking about getting her own place. She says Dad disapproves of everyone she dates. It's true. He thinks she's still his baby girl. Last week while on vacation, she went to stay with Dad's sister, who lives in Rensselaer, New York. While there, she went across the bridge to Albany, which is the state capital. She likes the city, and she visits every chance she gets. While visiting, she takes the opportunity to apply for two jobs. Lorraine comes home that weekend excited at the possibility of finding a job and moving to the city. A few days later, one of our cousins comes by to tell her she has gotten both jobs. With this news, Mom and Dad know they have to agree because she is already all but gone.

She agrees to stay with Dad's sister until she finds her own apartment, and with that, Mom and Dad reluctantly help her with the move. She comes home on weekends. I don't know about them, but I never get over her leaving. She is a kind, soft-spoken, gentle, playful big sister who always makes me feel safe. I recall that she taught me to play softball. For as long as I can remember, whenever the kids play ball, Lorraine is our designated pitcher. One day, when we are alone playing catch, she asks me if I can keep a secret. Not sure what a secret is, I say yes. She explains that playing ball is fun but winning is a matter of control. She spends weeks teaching me to pitch. Then, she teaches me to pitch with control. She says teams win or lose based on their pitcher's control. Little by little, she lets me pitch, when all the kids play ball. She is so right; when I don't pitch well, we lose.

Eventually, I learn to enjoy winning. I keep her secret because there is no reason to tell them why they can't win and why we can't lose. I'm not telling you that I am good. The only way I ever learned is, Lorraine has Mom's patience, and she would not give up on me. She smiles and tells me, "You can do this because you are smarter than I am. You will figure it out." She uses one of Dad's bushel baskets. She cut the bottom out of it and nails it to the back of the garage. I practice with the basket for years. Every time she comes home, she shows me something new to practice and learn. No matter what I tell her I want to try, she just smiles and says, "Just the way you learned to pitch, you will learn this. All you have to do is concentrate and practice, practice, practice." I recall that she taught me to decorate pretty Christmas trees, to draw, to sew, and to do my nails and hair. Lorraine is the person who taught me patience, faith, and control. I don't know who I would have become without her guiding hands and loving heart. Sisters truly are the greatest when they spend their lives loving you.

A few years pass, then one Sunday, Lorraine comes home, but on this occasion, she is not alone. She introduces her boyfriend to everyone and in a matter of fact fashion, states her intention to marry him. John is as clean as Clark Gable and as smooth as glass. He gets along with everyone and because he makes her happy, everyone including Dad puts forth a special effort to make him feel welcome. The next summer, John takes a job in St. Louis, wherever that is. All I know is it's more than a short bus ride away, and Dad is quietly irate. Being a true lady, woman, and mate, Lorraine follows her love to St. Louis. After two extremely hot summers and two even colder winters, Lorraine calls one night to say she is moving back home. I don't know what happened out there, but if she isn't happy there, I will be more than happy to have her home. It is winter here in upstate New York. It has been snowing all day, and there is almost three feet of snow covering everything. Margaret and I dress for the North Pole and walk to Western Union to wire her the money to come home. Margaret and I are seniors in high school. We were studying for midterm exams when Lorraine calls. All I know is, Mom doesn't ask any questions, and this time we don't even speak to Lorraine on the phone. I recall asking Mom when Lorraine will be home. Mom doesn't sound happy. Years later, Mom tells me she was unhappy that John would try to hit Lorraine. I ponder that word "try" for weeks. Three days pass by, and it is now Sunday. Our exams are over; so, Margaret and I went to church and then to the movies.

We come home in the early evening, surprised and delighted to find Lorraine waiting for us. From that moment on, home is really home again. For too long, I had missed hearing her leave for work at 5:30 a.m. in the morning, or hearing the ball game playing on the TV in her room. I miss hearing her laugh at something on TV. Mom and Lorraine are always a special pair. Lorraine will do anything for Mom. They go everywhere together and do everything together especially Major League ball games.

Lorraine never mentions John once, and no one dares invade her special space by asking. But that word "try" still haunts me. How do you try to hit someone? There has to be a funny story here, and I want to hear it. In the evening, I always go into her room, tell her jokes and funny stories, play cards, and otherwise annoy her until she asks Mom to make me leave her alone. That's just how she is. She never gets angry with me or put me out. She would tell Mom the way she did when I was little. When I ask her why she does that, she says, "I don't have any kids, but you are getting out of here."

Knowing she is serious, I leave her alone for now. As I think back, it was one of those nights when I ask her to explain something to me. She agrees, and with that I say, "Mom tells me that John tried to hit you. What does that mean?"

She looks at me for a very long minute and then replies, "I'm going to answer this question. But when I do, I don't ever want to talk about this subject again. Okay!"

I agree, and this is her answer.

"Pretty (old) boy John didn't want to work," she explains, "He would get and lose jobs just to keep from working. When John lost his last job, he then went out drinking with the guys. He comes home after having too many drinks and angry with himself, now yet, looking to vent his anger on someone else. That night, I decided not to be the one. John starts one of those one man arguments. When I tell him, 'I don't want to hear you.' That is enough reason for him to hit me." She continues, "He raises his hand and doesn't say 'Amen'; so, I assume he was going to hit me."

She says she caught his hand on the way down and bent his index finger backward until she heard a crack. She says that took all the anger and fight out of him. Now, he is sober and sorry. She says she then realized that he will never grow up and be responsible. And that's why I'm here answering your questions."

His lack of control made it impossible for them to win that game. I am truly sorry for her pain, yet again, she has taught me something new.

She looks at me, as only she can, and says, "Go ahead and laugh silly. I did!" And I did!

WELL, FOLKS

Well, folks, the kids are all grown up and doing their thing. Mom and Lorraine are watching the game on the big screen. They have the best seats in the house. So this seems like a good time to take my nap. I'm still trying to grow, but we will meet again somewhere between the sheets of another good book. Until then, this is Mom's fifth seed saying, "It's real."

Thank you, Mama!

About the Author

I'm Cynthia Ann, and I am my parents' fifth child, hence, the fifth seed. As my mother's third daughter, I am charmed and honored that she gave me her most prized possession: her name. Home for us was a small town in upstate New York. They call it Glasco, but I call it God's country—a friendly small, little place nestled between the mountains and the river. Mimicking my parents and siblings, I grew into an easy spirit. I own my soul. It keeps me walking in the sand while reaching for the heavens. A generous, always-forgiving God lives in my temple. Adorned with many talents, dreams, and desires passed down through generations, I am truly blessed.

It was in junior college that I first recognized the satisfying freedom that I derived from writing. Words flow easily, and my imagination knows no boundaries. Words fill me with understanding and peace.

I had to write this book! I needed to find a place for a lifetime of loving, caring, and sharing. It is imperative that I internalize what had always been external flesh and blood. I was breathing, yet I was no longer alive. My mind, heart, and spirit were in shock and dying in grief. I outlined then wrote my way from the past to the present. Somewhere between the pages, the pain decreased, and the joy for life increased. I have reached a place where I can think back and enjoy the blessing of Mama's words and deeds through all of my life.

I endeavored to select my favorite story of each family member that garnered laughter, insight, courage, progress, or care. These stories are shared by a baby whose existence in the genetic history of my family comes to life as Mama's fifth seed.

It is my observation that unity, structure, personal faith, discipline, and humor equal to family. I learned that home is unlike any other place you will ever know. Good, bad, or indifferent is yours.

I guarantee you fond memories; laughter; tantalizing, vivid, descriptive visualization of people, places, and of special times with Mama and the family.

These are the people you need to meet. In these stressful times, a soulful offering of peace and pleasure are the most welcome experience.

I am the most blessed woman I know, bar none, and I am eternally grateful.

Designed by : Manolito B. Bastasa

Reviewed by : Floramie Tuastomban

Date : October 28, 2005